CROSSING THE MAINSTREAM

CROSSING THE MAINSTREAM

New Fiction By Women Writers

Edited By Ann E. Larson and Carole A. Carr

Silverleaf Press
Seattle, Washington

Printed in the United States of America.

Text and cover design by Ann E. Larson and Carole A. Carr.
Cover photograph by Kathleen Pease, Copyright © 1975.

We gratefully acknowledge *Plainswoman, The Mill Hunk Herald,* and *Common Lives/Lesbian Lives* for permission to reprint previously published material as noted below.

Library of Congress Catalog Card Number: 86-63676
ISBN: 0-941121-01-1

First Edition, April 1987

CONTENTS

INTRODUCTION

Crossing The Mainstream began with a call for short stories about women with non-traditional lives. We meant non-traditional in a very broad sense – anything other than what society tells women they should be doing (or shouldn't be doing). We had a vision of an anthology of stories of diverse women – with jobs, relationships, attitudes, politics, living situations outside of the majority-defined "norm." Most of the stories we received were stories of the heart, about areas that have always been important to women: families, mother-daughter relationships, lovers' relationships, working, raising children, giving birth, not giving birth, and dying.

What makes this collection different is the choices these women make and the lives they live. Because they are different or are perceived as different, they sometimes face a hostile world. Having stepped outside the mainstream, they are in a sense on their own and must learn to define themselves. These women may also live with convolutions of traditional relationships, many have lesbian relationships, and some create their own communities.

Crossing The Mainstream is an affirmation for many who feel left out of the mass-market world. It is also an acknowledgement that if it is sometimes hard to do what is expected of you, it is often harder to do something different. What is the price for a woman to be herself? In these honest and insightful stories we find out; these women are real, their lives and quandaries, their joys and their pain.

Although three of the stories have appeared in literary magazines, the rest have not been published before. We are pleased to present *Crossing The Mainstream* as a collection of new fiction, a chance for new voices to be heard.

Silverleaf is an independent feminist press, committed to publishing quality fiction. We are very proud of this collection, our first book, and we are sure you will find it good reading. We want to thank all the writers who sent us material and our friends and supporters who believed in this book and in Silverleaf Press. We appreciate your support and welcome your comments.

Ann E. Larson and Carole A. Carr,
December 1986.

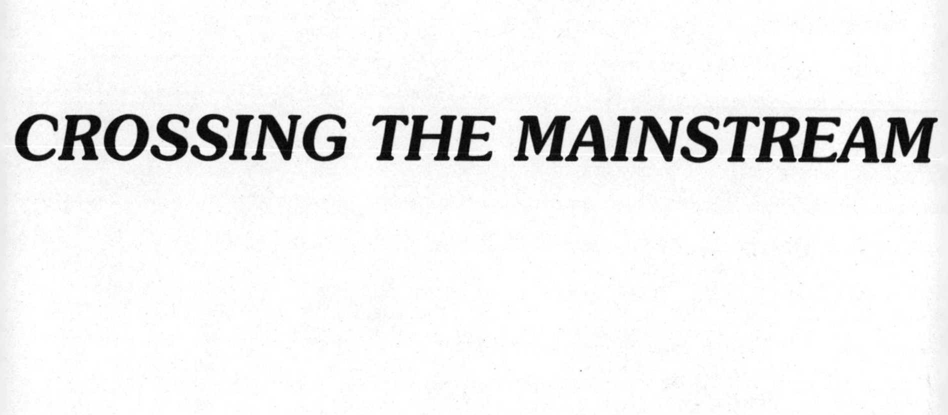

CROSSING THE MAINSTREAM

RHEA'S DAUGHTER

RUTHANN ROBSON

THEY SIT AMONG THE OTHER MOTHERS AND DAUGHTERS in the Women's Health Center Clinic. The mothers' faces pasty as cornstarch used to thicken their Thanksgiving gravy. The daughters' faces masked as the sequined princesses they once were some long ago Hallowe'en. The boyfriend or two sprinkled stiffly among the women have faces as if there will never be another holiday.

It is Saturday. The physician is on duty. Abortion day.

Caroline looks at her mother, almost unconsciously comparing her to the other mothers in the small room. Younger than most. Thick short hair that would have happily curled if it were half an inch longer. Too much jewelry. Olive skin. A husky woman in an Indian print dress. Peasant fingers.

The volunteer calls the last name "Hoffmann" several magazines after the scheduled appointment. Caroline and her mother rise, looking for the completed forms on the clipboard. Caroline watches as her mother slides through the door, clutching papers to her chest like a shield. If the other inhabitants of the waiting room are surprised that it is the older woman who goes into the physician's chambers, they do not dwell on their reactions to outsiders.

AT FORTY, COOKIE is going to have a simple surgical procedure. Nothing to it. It will be completed as her daughter Caroline sits and reads magazines. Cookie looks at her forms: her health history (no allergies, no hemophilia), her reproductive history (one child still living, no previous abortions or miscarriages) and her menstruation cycles (usually regular, last period 16 weeks ago). The facts of her body's life swim before her in her own handwriting. But what seems most odd is her own name: Rhea Hoffmann.

Rhea. Her given name. The name she never used except on her driver's license, her insurance policies. A Greek name. She'd heard her father was Greek, but she didn't know him and didn't know his name, either first or last. Yet she'd always assumed her father named her Rhea, perhaps because her mother never used it, always calling her Cookie. And everyone else had always called her Cookie, until when asked her name, she said "Cookie" without thinking. Sometimes people even laughed when they heard her real name. Only Caroline had said it was beautiful, that it was the name of a powerful goddess. But Caroline had always been a bit offbeat, even as a child. A child with her head either in the clouds or in a book. A child to worry over, which Cookie did religiously.

CAROLINE STILL FEELS THE VIBRATING MOTION of the car. It was a nine hour drive. But when Cookie called, Caroline always came. Who else was there? In some sense, Caroline always felt as if she were the mother rather than the daughter. Condescending as she knew it was, Caroline saw her mother needing her more than she needed her mother. But Caroline felt that way about most people.

Yet without debating, Caroline dropped her life and headed north from Key West. Up to Orlando, Florida. Home of

Disney World. Home of sinkholes. Home of Martin-Marietta, where Caroline's father worked as a draftsman. Caroline had stopped imagining her father drawing little lines on graph paper, a harmless design that would one day find its way into a bomb. Caroline's standard of living had risen and fallen with the tide of defense contracts for almost nineteen years.

THE LIGHTS SEEM TOO BRIGHT in the room to Cookie as she changes into a greenish dressing gown that feels like a bargain brand paper towel. She tries not to think. I have no choice. No choice. She repeats the phrase to herself, echoing her own incantation. No choice.

At first, she had not believed in her own pregnancy. A child at forty? Impossible. Just the change of life she supposed. But the feeling tugged familiarly: the gagging during breakfast, the difficulty in waking up each morning. She recognized this ever present wave of nauseous weariness. It became impossible to deny. A child. That man's child. No choice.

She called her only child, Caroline. Her daughter. A mother's only true friend. One who loved unconditionally. One who never judged.

CAROLINE READS ANOTHER GLAMOUR ARTICLE, "How to Look Like a Million on Ninety-Seven Dollars." Mix and match was the secret. The same secret she'd read seven or eight years ago, probably in this same magazine, while sitting on the beach with her mother. She had tried to imagine herself a slick career girl, sitting at a desk with important papers she would call "documents." That was her fantasy when she was trying to be practical. When she abandoned the prudence of her class and gave herself to the lull of the ocean, she saw herself as a doctor. A physician among the poor of India; Appalachia; Africa. A savior with no need for coordinated clothes.

Caroline knew her mother didn't have the same fantasies for her daugher as Caroline had for herself. Caroline knew

Cookie's fantasies included the love of a rich man who would worship both Caroline and Cookie. They would all live in a big house, happily ever after, Caroline eternally devoted to Cookie. But when Caroline left home for some obscure Alabama college on a scholarship, Cookie's dreams broke around her daughter like cheap Christmas ornaments, slivering into Caroline's will. "This is the thanks I get. I raise you. I deny myself everything. I do without for years. Then you just up and leave. I ruined my life for you. I should have had a damn abortion."

Caroline noted to herself that abortions were illegal then. She hardened into a person who could leave home and make her way in the world. But she vowed never to forgive her mother. Not in a million years.

COOKIE LOOKS AT THE DOCTOR, his face pale and round as a New England harvest moon. His green scrub smock makes his skin look even more jaundiced. Cookie has seen kids on the street wearing similar shirts: playing at being doctors, she supposed. But this was no game. This is real. The consequences of everything Cookie has ever done seem to choke her. Some strain of Catholicism she thought long ago stamped out rises in her throat. She begins to pray to the Virgin Mary. **Mother of God, I have sinned. Mother of God, have mercy.**

"So, young lady, why did you wait so long? You've made things a bit more difficult for us." The doctor's voice, yellowed at the edges, seeps into Cookie's fear. She sees the needle. She hears the doctor again, trying to be soothing in a sarcastic sort of way. She squeezes her eyes closed tight as they will go. **Get me through this.** She thinks about how different her life would have been if only she were a dancer.

HOW TO CHOOSE YOUR DOCTOR. Another mindless article. Caroline barely notices that all the patient pronouns are feminine and all the doctor pronouns are masculine. She does read the subsection on 'The New Woman Doctor' which covers two paragraphs. The advice is not to choose a doctor simply on the basis of *her* sex. Other factors are more important.

It seems very long ago to Caroline that she had wanted to be a doctor. Caroline Hoffmann, M.D. She'd changed her projected specialties often: internal medicine, ophthalmology, neurology, dermatology, orthopedics and even hematology. But never pediatrics. Never gynecology.

Four years at an experimental college had altered Caroline's perspective. She began to view modern medicine as a province of the patriarchy, with its severings and sutures and surgeries. She became interested in holistic health. She studied herbalism. Still, she had taken the MCATs for the hell of it. Performed respectably, but not outstanding enough to attract a scholarship. So, she concluded that though she wanted to be a doctor, she didn't want it badly enough. She never wanted anything badly enough. Or so she judged herself.

COOKIE IS TRYING NOT TO FEEL anything, but it seems to her that she can. The room spins. Voices grow cloudy. She must focus her mind. Focus. She thinks about dancing. Dancing. Her body is not horizontal. She is vertical, leaping and vertical. She is in a room with mirrors watching herself jeté across the resined floor. Jeté. Jeté. Tour jeté.

CAROLINE WONDERS WHAT SILK OAK WOULD THINK of the collection of women in this room. Probably pity, giving way to political rhetoric. Sometimes Caroline thought Silk Oak really didn't understand the hardships of the world; she was so childlike. Caroline had told Silk Oak that her mother had called and that she had to go see her. But Caroline didn't relate the contents of her mother's raging telephone conversation. Some things are better not discussed, even with one's lover; especially with one's lover. Besides, perhaps if Caroline didn't tell anyone, it wouldn't be true. She knew Cookie's proclivity for exaggeration.

Still, how did one exaggerate being pregnant? Caroline remembered the Greeks used wallflower, but it wasn't reliable. It was too late for pennyroot. So Caroline searched her books for a good herbal abortifacient. But her volumes either ignored the subject or treated it as a crime. One of her most trusted guides stated, "Herbal abortives have purposely been overlooked. I consider them dangerous." More dangerous than some surgeon's knife? Caroline wondered. After all, this was her *mother* she was thinking about.

COOKIE HAS STOPPED DANCING. She is sinking. Sinking into the wooden floor of the ballroom. She will never be able to move her legs again, she thinks. She is sinking.

CAROLINE'S LEGS GLOW GREENISH TAN in the fluorescent lights of the waiting room, two radioactive limbs of flesh sticking out from her white shorts. The same shorts she wore in her mother's kitchen, the day before yesterday.

"You shouldn't wear white when you travel." Her mother seemed to make a smooth transition from talking about the arrangements to commenting on Caroline's attire.

"Not that it matters, but it isn't Daddy's, is it?" This was more of a statement than a question. Caroline hoped both that it was and that it wasn't.

When Cookie told Caroline of the young black man responsible for the growth in her, Caroline nodded. When Cookie said she didn't even know the guy's name, Caroline asked her mother if she had been raped. Cookie was indignant, as if such a thing could never happen to her.

Caroline was left alone at the kitchen table, the burnt aftertaste of her own racism forming lumps on her tongue. Her foot drew circles on the blue linoleum floor. Circles of sadness. For her mother's loneliness. For the fact that her father had never been enough for her mother. For the marriage of her parents, still enduring despite the countless secret affairs that everyone knew about.

COOKIE IS BELOW the wooden floor of the mirrored room. No one dances here.

SHE SHOULD HAVE BROUGHT A BOOK, but nothing seemed suitable. What does one read while waiting for one's mother to have an abortion? Nothing funny. Nothing with impact. Nothing requiring even a shred of concentration. Magazines. Caroline gets another Glamour from the rack in the waiting room, trying not to imagine what is happening on the other side of the partitioned walls. The doctor must be vacuuming and cutting some *thing* from her mother's womb, from the very same spot she had so desperately clung to over twenty years ago.

Yet Caroline has difficulty visualizing herself as an embryo, though she's seen countless pictures of these fuzzy creatures. Even more difficult is the task of thinking of herself as desperate. Did she really cling to life? Four weeks late being delivered, did she ever want to be born? She remembers at nine, wishing aloud that she were dead. "Don't be dramatic," her friend had said. But Caroline knew she'd meant it, though she never said it again. It became a clenched knot in her stomach. Her very own secret.

THE NURSE LOOKS DOWN AT THE WOMAN BLEEDING on the narrow table. Older than most of the other patients. Old enough to know better, she thinks, though quickly adds, better than what? The nurse views herself as inhabiting some muted shade between realism and cynicism. The blood soaking the double sheets on the table seems to the nurse to be the price one pays for looking for love. Or part of the price.

It is almost over now. The nurse realizes the woman has given herself over to blankness, unconsciousness. The red river of blood is eddied with mucous. As the nurse is already plunging the needle into Cookie's limp arm, the doctor orders an IV prepared. It is over. The nurse cleans up.

CAROLINE SLOWLY ALLOWS HERSELF to miss Silk Oak. Right now, she thinks, Silk Oak is probably watching the cats roll in the island sun. She hopes Silk Oak misses her, or is at least painfully conscious of her absence. Caroline can't imagine Silk Oak outside of her own presence.

She never told Silk Oak much about her mother. She never told anyone much about her mother. For Caroline thought that Cookie's life was solely Cookie's possession, Cookie's secret. Caroline never thought of her mother as her *own* secret. For Caroline worked hard at maintaining the facade that she and her mother were two entirely separate and independent beings.

"GET HER FRIEND IN THE WAITING ROOM," the nurse tells the volunteer. The volunteer has a good memory for pairing people and walks over to Caroline.

"You're Rhea Hoffman's friend?"

"I'm her daughter." Caroline goes pale. Her mother is dead, she just knows it. She follows the volunteer automatically, into the second small room on the left. She sees her mother, a tube in her arm, gagging. The nurse is holding a small flat plastic container near Cookie's twisted head. Cookie is gagging up a yellowish bile. She had not eaten for twelve hours, just as instructed, but still she vomits a stream of some xanthic liquid.

Caroline strokes her mother's flat hair and finds herself holding the plastic container. Cookie is still retching. "You'll be all right." Caroline tries to remember a collection of soothing sounds, a mantra, anything. But all she can say is "It's all right."

THE TWO WOMEN DRIVE TOWARDS HOME in a silence punctuated only by Caroline alternating "Are you all right?" with "It's all right" at every stop light, every corner. The ride seems to take hours. Caroline sees streets she never noticed before. She keeps feeling as if she is lost. The traffic is ungodly. Caroline faintly realizes that it is late Saturday afternoon. The Altamonte Mall, with its one hundred and six specialty stores and three major department stores, is strewing cars into the road, clogging her way. She wants only to get home. Home.

But the mall traffic is a whirlpool around her, pulling her down. The hours she had spent in that cave now seemed so wasted. In high school she worked at the book store there, Walden's. She'd stolen at least one book for every hour she worked, reasoning she was underpaid. Then there was the Oriental shop, where she'd spent her lunch hours looking at quilted jackets and carved boxes, trying on dresses. Has this mall really been here that long, Caroline wonders. Has it always been this far away from home?

ONCE IN THE HOUSE, Caroline guides Cookie into the bedroom and then into a nightgown. She gets a fresh Kotex for her from the closet and rolls the old soaked one up in toilet paper. "Sleep," she says to her mother.

In the back yard, Caroline puts the wrapped Kotex into a thick green trash bag along with the blue print Indian dress. "Wear something loose," they had told Cookie, "no pants." So Caroline had given her mother the only dress she'd brought, a thin cotton blue one. There's nothing wrong with the dress now, but Caroline is certain Cookie will never want to see the dress again. Caroline certainly never wants to see it again.

SUNDAY MORNING, COOKIE lies in bed wanting to be asleep as her daughter sprawls around the small house. At least her husband is gone for the weekend, hunting deer in some swamp. No accident, of course. Cookie planned it all.

Cookie does not feel as much pain as she thinks she should. Only cold clamped aches. Only a wetness that seems like it will never stop. Six weeks. No sex. No swimming. No baths. No tampons. Cookie thinks that the tampons will be the most difficult thing to do without.

Cookie tries to relax into sleep, but she listens for Caroline's sounds in the other room. All those nights spent listening for Caroline's sounds: cries, gurgles, breathing, coughing or even a too long silence that might signal that something was wrong. Cookie had loved that child like she loved nothing else. Her daughter. And she'd vowed her child would grow up with a mother who loved her. Not with a woman like Cookie's own mother, whose jealousies and regrets made her treat her daughter like a stranger. No, Caroline would always know she was the most precious thing on earth to her mother.

YOU COULD ALWAYS CHANGE YOUR NAME, or so Caroline heard. That would solve a lot of problems. Get a new identity. Silk Oak was always advocating some new name for Caroline. But more fortuitous numerological consequences notwithstanding, Caroline declined to change her name. Even her last name. "It's not my father's name," she'd told Silk Oak, "it's my name." Silk Oak had just shook her head, impatient as if Caroline were a slow learning child.

When Silk Oak had discovered that Caroline's mother's name was Rhea, she got out her mythology dictionary and decided that Caroline should change her name to Hera, one of the daughters of Rhea. Caroline reminded Silk Oak that Hera had been raped by Zeus, married him and then constantly fought Zeus as well as his countless and mortal lovers and his numerous offspring. None of that was anything Caroline wanted to identify with.

"Then take it as a last name," Silk Oak persisted. "Would you deny your mother? The matrilineal line?"

Caroline had gathered her silence closer. Yes, she would.

Not for money or power, not even for love, but to maintain some core that she thought of as herself, as Caroline, she would deny her mother and all her foremothers. A million times.

COOKIE LIFTS HERSELF from the bed to go to the bathroom for another Kotex, passing Caroline sitting at the kitchen table reading. Caroline always looks like she's waiting for something, Cookie thinks briefly.

"How you feeling, Ma?"

"O.K." Cookie leaves the bathroom door open. She packs two sanitary pads between her thighs and limps back toward the table.

"Sit down, Ma. You want some coffee? Some tea? Some milk or juice? A glass of water?" Caroline rushes her words around her mother's sallow apparition.

"No. I'm fine."

The two women sit in silence. Cookie puts her head down on the table. She feels incredibly weary.

CAROLINE FEELS FROZEN NUMB around her mother. She usually finds herself searching for things to say anyway, but this is impossible. What can you say in a situation like this? Perhaps Glamour should run an article, "Eighty-seven comforting things to say to your mother after she's had an abortion." The best kept secret of all.

To cope, Caroline directs her mind to wander away. To anything at all. Anything other than this. The articles in Glamour she'd read yesterday. The ads in Glamour. The whole idea of having a magazine for women called Glamour. Glamour was what the witches had; the power to cast a spell. What the witches were burned for.

COOKIE WANTS TO TALK, but Caroline seems so alien sometimes. She wants her daughter's comfort. She wants to explain everything.

"I'm so lonely." Cookie looks at her daughter's legs stretched sideways on the chair. "You really should shave yourself. Your legs are disgusting; all those clumps of hair."

Caroline shrugs. Silent.

"I'm just trying to *help* you." Cookie winces as if she's been insulted. "I'm so damn lonely. Your father is always off working or hunting and when he's home, I wish he'd get the hell out of here. He sits in front of that damn TV like a lump of dogshit, then looks at *me* funny when I go out. What does he expect? *He* won't talk to me.

"But I'll tell you one damn thing, I'll be more careful next time. I'm not going through this again. You can't imagine how awful it is. You just can't imagine. At least you'll never have to go through this. You're lucky. You live with a bunch of women down there. I'd do that too, but I can't stand those clumps of hair on their legs. And they'd probably want me to be the man."

Caroline's face does not flicker behind her sixth grade sequined mask.

CAROLINE ESCAPES FROM HER MOTHER by taking the dog for a walk. Rusty. Good old convenient Rusty. A few blocks away and she is out from under the spell of silence cast by her mother. She begins to tick off advice: Don't count on others for your happiness, search in your own spirit. Change your diet, get rid of all that sugar. Make a career move.

The reason Caroline didn't say such things to her mother was not because she lacked nerve; but because she realized how stupid all these curt cliches sounded. And she didn't have faith in their truth. Sometimes Caroline wishes she were more like Silk Oak, who thought that the cure for everything that ailed a woman was to throw off the yoke of patriarchy and become a separatist. But it seemed to Caroline that the reason women let men damage them was that they'd been damaged by women, who'd been damaged themselves. When it came to blame, Caroline thought that the apportionment could never be straightforward. There were too many players.

UNLEASHING THE DOG, back in the kitchen, Caroline finds Cookie exactly where she'd left her, only now her mother was swirling a cup of coffee with an Oreo.

"How you doing, Ma?" Caroline studies her mother's sturdy face for clues.

"All right. I'm still a little dizzy, though. What's that ax on your neck?"

Caroline picks up the silver ornament on a chain around her neck. It was a present from Silk Oak and had been made by a woman in Boston, probably one of Silk Oak's former lovers, though Caroline wasn't quite sure. Caroline looks at the charm as if she has never seen it before.

"It's a labrys," she finally says. "A double ax. Symbol of the Amazons."

"Aren't those the crazy women that eat men?" Cookie asks. Without waiting for an answer, Cookie adds, "It's stupid." She has never been a woman to sugar coat her truths.

IN THE CAR, DRIVING SOUTH, Caroline is not exactly sure how she got here. There was always something in Cookie's dark eyes that let Caroline know her mother wanted to be rid of her. And if the eyes weren't enough, Cookie had said, "Well, you'd better get back to your girlfriend and your herbs." She began to gather Caroline's things. Then there was the quick kiss on the cheek and the requisite sarcastic Princess Caroline remark, as if Cookie herself had not named her daughter. Then Caroline finds herself safely tucked in her car, shifting gears.

When she gets on the Florida Turnpike, Caroline indulges in some breathing exercises to calm herself. She is angry. Angry at her mother's alternating self pity and arrogance. But more angry that her mother doesn't appreciate her. She drove all this way to help her mother out of another fix and all she gets is criticism. Don't wear white to travel. Shave your legs. Your necklace is stupid. Caroline is exceeding the speed limit by almost twenty miles per hour and the Volkswagen is shaking.

SHE GETS HOME AFTER DARK. The bugs ooze through the kitchen, not even bothering to scramble when she turns on the light. Silk Oak has not taken the garbage outside and has not kept the food scraps in the refrigerator as Caroline always does. No one is home. The phone is ringing. Caroline debates whether or not to answer it: somebody must want something. She feels as though she can't give another thing, but she moves toward the bedroom phone.

"Hello."

"Hello. It's your mother. I'm glad you got back safely. Listen, I just wanted to thank you for coming up to be with me."

"That's OK. Are you feeling all right?"

"Yeah. I'd better hang up. Your father will kill me with all these long distance calls."

There is nothing gradual about the disconnecting click of a telephone.

CAROLINE SCOOPS UP ARTEMIS, her favorite cat, and sits on the back porch steps in the dark. The flowers from the yard smell especially sweet. The herb garden's familiar smell is soothingly pungent. It is good to be home. Where she almost belongs. Remembering that Silk Oak won't be home until after midnight from her waitress job, Caroline decides to go for a walk. Out to the edge of the canal. Out to the calm shadows of the Caribbean. Still carrying Artemis, Caroline wanders through the hibiscus and buttonwood. She strokes the cat and looks at the clear gibbous moon.

Tomorrow is the vernal equinox. Spring. Tomorrow she and Silk Oak will meet some of the other women in their community down by the old beach path. Tomorrow all the women will sing an ancient song. Tomorrow one of the women will tell the myth of Demeter and Persephone and everyone will dance in celebration of Persephone's return. Tomorrow. Rhea's daughter begins to cry.

CHILDCARE

MARIAN MICHENER

JULY 14, OLYMPIC FOREST, WITH THE KID

The Kid: Kate's Joy. She is fine. Her bones are fine. Her face is fine. She is so fine she is almost transluscent. She is four and a half feet tall and seven years old and you can see when something's about to come out of her mouth before it arrives.

I guess I've loved her ever since the morning she wandered into Kate's room soft as bedclothes and found me there and buried her face in her mother's freckled shoulder until she was ready to meet me. For a long time then, I loved her as an extension of Kate: touched her as a way of touching Kate, entertained her to entertain Kate.

Today, the whole drive up from Portland, she played Nancy Drew. "A woman has mysteriously disappeared. We have to find her."

I asked her, "What does she look like? Where was she last seen?" And I could see invention turning as she put her finger to her temple.

"Tall and thin. . . About thirty."

And blonde with long fingers and a tic at the corner of her tricky blue eyes when she's nervous, I thought, sure she was describing her mother. I didn't think we would find her on this trip.

"She left a message. She had a lead on the mystery of the lost castle and she was going to the forest."

An obvious red herring. I had all but solved for myself any mystery about Kate's whereabouts, but Joy's plot fit our plan for the weekend, so I said, "We better get there as fast as we can."

She trained a bloodhound gaze on the passing scenery where even the quiver of powerlines was a clue. "Hmm," she would repeat, "I wonder."

Olympic Forest: We walked in late in the afternoon through light filtered down in slanting columns. I'm sitting against a cedar log and the pain in my chest is rising with the campfire and spreading thin where the sky is above the trees. Joy took a few pages from my book to write a journal of her own. But just now she's wandering over tangled roots and putting her face against the Ponderosa to smell the vanilla bark.

As I was oiling my boots this evening with all the love I love to do that with, I told her, "With these boots I can do anything."

And she sassed back, "Huh-uh," and spilled her hot chocolate.

I handed her a bandana and asked, "What? What can't I do with these boots?"

"Tap dance," she said, and she put down her cup to demonstrate a few steps cracking cool needles with her bare feet. Then she twirled around the clearing and laughed, bowl-cut brown hair following her head to settle a moment after she settled into a pose of stillness.

Staking the tarp this evening, I composed some smug postcard to my father who took the boys backpacking when I was Joy's age and left me home kicking weeds. That was the year before he packed out altogether. I do not think he knows this trail.

He stopped by last week and filled the doorway with treats and concerns the way he does every once in a while. He mutely offers champagne and roses and I dutifully hug him across the threshhold, though he feels like a parking meter in my arms. I love the way it surprised him to find Joy there making out our camping list. She looked a little offended and I thought we shared a swift understanding that fathers will show up just when things are getting fun and expect to be paid attention to. He lifted one shag eyebrow to ask who she was, and I wished I knew him well enough to say: this is a branch with roots deep in my heart, old man, the closest you'll ever come to a granddaughter, and she's got a world of possibilities ahead of her that you can't even imagine and I can hardly wait to see. Instead I said, "This is Joy."

Bastille Day: The first time Kate and I made love she said it was like a wall had fallen down. I thought she meant the wall between her and the place where women reach inside each other until they touch themselves. But life turns out to be full of these dams and floods. And the fantasy of the liberator is its own punishment. Tonight I'm sure she's with her new joshua and I am the wall that's crumbling.

Where is my litany against jealousy? There is that zen saying: if you would keep your cow, give her the world as her pasture. A woman is not a cow, but I suppose it follows that if I give my lover her joshua, she can't betray my faith. But I'm not even sure we're lovers anymore and the fire is down and the light is going and I can't see any more words.

JULY 16, WEST OF HURRICANE RIDGE, WITH JOY

I had walking on my mind this morning, but Joy was scrunched into the bottom of her sleeping bag silent and intractable. After all of yesterday I thought she might be tired, but when I tried to scratch her back and say, "Okay, sleep in," she wriggled away.

"Mosquitoes," she said to her knees.

I coaxed her out and counted the colonies of bites on her back and shoulders. I teased her for treating the bastards to such a feast. She itched and sniffed and retreated to the foot of her bag, but not before I slathered calomine all over and pressed a few gulps of springwater on her. I boiled some oatmeal and mixed in the prize salmonberries she hunted in the brush yesterday. She has her way of turning food and rest into wide-ranging energy and she should recover soon. Meanwhile, I have a little time to write.

Yesterday, she was up before I was and we walked all day through thick green that massaged our eyes and air so sweet we could have eaten it for dessert. A sunny day in the rainforest means enjoying the growth without paying its price. Two deer with eyes like Joy's met us on the path, munched thoughtfully on the sight of us, then kicked and faded in the woods.

There was a campsite beside a gray pool with a snowmelt waterfall emptying into it and out of it. To get there, we had to cross a fallen log ten feet over a fair rush of river. The girl detective balked at this. "Do we have to walk on the log?"

I wasn't sure. We sat against our packs and ate dates and sunflower seeds and watched the mist snagging the top of the ridge. I bushwacked up and down the bank and came back to say there was no other way across, but that we could stay there or backtrack to another site.

She asked me, "If we cross the log, can I hold your hand?"

Bridges without rails, my own recurring nightmare. But I did have on my boots that can do anything. So I backed across the log ahead of her and she asked me not to take her hands unless she reached for me. She put out her arms for a tap dancer's balance and held my eyes instead. Only on the first foot of solid ground on the other side did we wrap our arms around each other while the sun fell toward the trees and her fear and my fear promised to take care of each other forever.

When camp was set, she tried to teach me to skip rocks on the pool—slowly, carefully demonstrating and explaining the necessary circles of hand and wrist. My rocks sank. Hers flew.

She wanted to pick berries from the hillside to take back to Kate who had taught her to leave two for the deer for every one she picked. I worked the other side of the path behind her so as not to undo this thoughtful arithmetic. We filled our water bottles with red and blue huckleberries and ate as many as we picked. I tried for the hard-to-reach ones and twice almost tumbled down the hill. When I asked, "Enough?" she said, "One more bend." And around the bend was an identical stretch of berry bushes, tree, sky and another bend. I asked, "One more bend?" and we urged each other around and up until we reached the top of the ridge just in time to see the sun go down over Desolation Point.

For some reason, sunsets and overlooks are no big deal to seven-year-olds. But she was patient with me as I watched and sighed and rubbed her shoulders in the cooling.

Walking back down with the night coming on, she pointed out the first star and I started to wish for love like I always do, but decided instead to wish for the strength to survive the love I already have.

Under half a moon and a million stars we watched the water spreading under the waterfall, circling through the pool and flowing on. I saw my love affair with Kate as a rock garden.

Contemplating the way we separate from domestic circles, I thought of my prodigal father – just when I was so satisfied that we had come to a place our fathers could never bring us even if they wanted to. For the first time in a long time I wanted to ask him something important, how to hold on as we pass on.

Something precious in the separation was that Joy was no longer my lover's daughter. We were two women children sitting by the water.

She told me a story about a magic waterfall that could talk and make itself invisible. When hunters came, or fire, the waterfall would warn all the small creatures of the woods and tell them to hide in its watery arms and then it would disappear with them until the danger was gone.

She's up now and so impatient with my writing that she has washed the oatmeal pan and begun to roll up her sleeping bag.

JULY 17, HOME

Delivered Joy home about midnight last night after our late start and a plodding hike out plus the habit I have of driving the limit when the kid is in the car. Relieved to feel hollow kissing Kate and shaking the hand of her stiffly smiling joshua (really his name is Mark).

Woke up aching in five distinct and varied joints, mouth dry as a library, phone ringing. It was Kate with her, "Good morning, beautiful," but I didn't feel much like either. She asked me over for huckleberry muffins. I asked her who was there. Just Mark, she said, because Joy's father had come early and taken her for the day.

I thought of something Joy had said that last night in the forest. She had been sitting nestled in my arms watching the water and I'd asked her was she ready to go to sleep. She'd said no and cocked her head to look up at the sky. After minutes of rushing water sounds and skinny shoulder blades breathing against my chest, she'd said, "Okay," and stood up and explained, "I just had to count a hundred stars first."

"Not today," I said to Kate. "Thanks."

I want to remember how, last night, after reuniting the nuc fam, I went to Alice B.'s and found a few friends there as usual. I carried on with them about the trees and the light and the deer and the waterfall and the pool and the berries and the sunset over the shore. Then, in the late night hush, I got a little maudlin over delicate connections dying and my doubts about how much more of Joy's life I'll be on hand to see. And I found about a half a dozen other single dykes with pictures in their wallets of the children of their hearts all over the world. We told their stories until the lights went out.

Something like the great blue heron that flew out from the canyon wall yesterday morning as we were leaving, a surprising certainty overtook me out on the empty street: that I was the disappearing woman, tall and thin and almost thirty, that Nancy Drew was tracking in the woods.

RITES OF PASSAGE

CAROLE A. CARR

I was sitting in the outside toilet singing, "Red Sails in the Sunset." I leaned back and lifted my head to get a better echo in that dismal space, and felt the key, which had been tied around my neck on a string, slide down my front to land with a plop in the water below. One quick glance confirmed my fear, the key was gone. And I hadn't unlocked the door to the house yet. This was the third key I had lost in a year. For the life of me I couldn't remember how I'd lost the other two. I tried to recall the threat which Mum had handed out with this last key but I couldn't remember that either. Mum said I was exasperating and that all I thought about was rock n' roll. She was wrong, though; all I thought about was rock n' roll and sex.

I padded out of the toilet and sat on the back steps of the house, stretched out my legs and surveyed my black slip-on shoes and fluorescent, hot-pink ankle socks. My spirits lifted somewhat. I was still young enough to be hit and Mum had a terrible temper, but my size was becoming my protection. I loomed above Mum, my schoolmates, and best of all, Rose. As I mentally reviewed the Top 10 I had heard on the radio the night before (the disc jockey, trying to sound American, exclaiming, "Here we are again, guys and gals, coming to you live from the Manchester Ballroom with the best from America for this 35th week of 1959") I heard a quick, low laugh coming from inside the house. I groaned, pulled up my knees and leaned my head against them. Rose was home. I was so dismayed at hearing her voice I didn't question why she was home. She and Mum usually didn't get home until after tea; they both worked as waitresses downtown.

Stretching out again, I thought about my sister, Rose. She had left the Secondary Technical school just as I started. Most of her life was a mystery to me. Her reputation, however, lingered on in school. When I showed up after Rose, there was a lot of whispering and people sort of hung around to see what I would do. It all died down pretty quick, though, when it became evident that Rose and I ran on different tracks. Rose did all right for herself, she did. She didn't just walk into class – she sort of oozed. She never knew what was going on academically, but who cared? I heard all the teachers, I mean the men, made bets as to how quick they could get something going. What happened was that Rose got going. Fed up, she decided to quit school and work as a waitress. I must admit, Mum did egg her on a bit. Sort of mercenary Mum is. As soon as Rose started pulling in a wage, Mum wanted 50% of it for "expenses." So far Rose was going along with this, but I wondered when she would decide to take off.

I was pulled up short in my thoughts. I heard Rose squeal and I shuddered. That was a bit much even for her. But she'd changed somehow, lately. She'd had her hair cut short and it curled black over her head and wisps lay about her neck and her ears. It made her look young and innocent. But I still hated her. The thing I hated most about Rose was her figure. She had one. What's more, she flaunted it in front of me every night, saying things like, "Let me know when you want to borrow my bra, Joan." Then she would flounce into the bathroom, snickering.

The truth was, if she ever caught me even thinking of borrowing something of hers, she would start screaming at me until her eyes bugged out. Everytime she did this, I would strut around the bedroom singing Mario Lanza's drinking song from the "Student Prince." There was a joke in our family about Rose's father being an Italian because she was dramatic and always screaming and waving her arms around. This was a bit stupid of me actually, because the stories about both of our fathers were a bit thick. Mostly Mum kept her mouth shut, but once in a while if she'd had a few she would drop hints. I swear it was no accident. I mean, we might have been accidents, but it was no accident that she dropped hints. She never told us the things that kids are supposed to hear. It was always, "You're old enough to know the truth," or, "You're old enough to take care of yourself."

I sank further into my daydreams and was almost asleep on the steps when I heard the door open. I moved to get up and a boy shot past me. Rose grabbed me and hustled me inside. Leaning against the door as she closed and locked it, she winked. The boy had looked rather dazed. Rose didn't. She was now grinning from ear to ear, and waving a pearl necklace from her left hand, she started dancing around the small kitchen, which was no easy task. I was dreading the moment when she'd make a grab for my hand so she could really let it rip. Rose never got the message that I couldn't jive – well, at least I couldn't in front of anybody. I pressed myself against the wall. "Here she comes," I was thinking when there was a banging at the front door. Like an echo, there was a knock at the back door. Peeking out the kitchen window I spied the dazed boy, now looking somewhat recovered, standing resolutely on the doorstep. "Get rid of him," hissed Rose, expertly applying fresh skiffle pink lipstick to her mouth, while shoving the pearl necklace into the knife and fork drawer. As I hesitated, she pushed me to the door and took off out of the kitchen and down the hall to the front door. I was used to getting rid of Rose's boyfriends and this one looked like no challenge. The hard ones were those who knew they weren't in love. In the beginning, I had nourished a vain hope that one of Rose's castoffs would seek comfort and revenge by choosing me. But it never happened. I had tried all kinds of things to attract her boys' attention, even Rose's lipstick and her periwinkle blue eyeshadow. All I got were odd stares from the boys and hell from Rose. I decided to give up on Rose's boys and find one of my own.

Reflecting on how uneven life was, I opened the door and peered around, while holding my body firmly behind it. I wore my long-suffering, "I'm just her little sister" look, which apparently this boy had encountered before. Giving me no guff, he backed disgustedly down the steps and disappeared around the side of the toilet. Sighing, I shut the door but didn't lock it just in case Rose became capricious again.

I walked past the livingroom, trying hard not to look or hear anything. Pulled hard by the silence, I peered around the door to the left where the couch was. All I could see was a tangle of legs hanging over the near end of the couch. Blushing, I crept upstairs to the bedroom Rose and I shared. We had pushed our beds into separate corners so that we could avoid each other as much as possible. Rose had even taken her nail polish and dabbed a line across the linoleum marking off her territory. Cross it and you're dead, she said. Of course I crossed it. I had to. We also shared a dresser. Or rather she loaned me the bottom two drawers and she had the top three plus the space on top of the dresser, which was piled up with heaps of make-up, nylons, and magazines. Over all was a fine layer of Max Factor powder which she would occasionally blow off when she needed to find something at the bottom of the pile.

My side of the room was covered in pictures of my "heartthrobs" as Mum called them. She knew that really got my goat. But secretly I swooned. Rick Nelson's picture was on the ceiling over my bed so that when I woke up I could look into his eyes. I had pictures of Fats Domino, Chuck Berry, The Everleys, Buddy Holly; all the greats from America on one wall with a special place reserved for Brenda Lee. Life was hard; I was secretly in love with Brenda but she wouldn't leave America.

My one consolation was Janet. She was the champion girl swimmer in our school. She was husky and blonde with shoulder muscles that made the boys gulp. Sometimes at night I would saunter up and down her street but she never came out. I don't know what I would have done if she had. Meanwhile, I had to deal with reality, which was how did I find a boy? The pressure was on at school, or at least in my class. Everyone was keeping a tally. So far, five girls had lost their virginity. They had done It. My Mum always referred to sex as "it." That's all she said – it – never said what we were supposed to do or not do with it.

I was thinking how it wasn't a problem at all for some girls, while I waited for my best friend Jean, on Saturday. I had sneaked a scarf off Rose's dresser and Jean was going to tie it for me. I was scared about going to the Arcade but it was the place to be on a Saturday afternoon. It was where Connie and Rita hung out and I was a little afraid of them even though we had all gone through school together. They went to the Arcade to pick up boys and the boys they usually picked up were from the Poulton Reform School. Saturday afternoon was when they let them out. These boys were tough. They smoked a lot and pushed up the sleeves of their jackets so you could see their tattoos. The Arcade was packed. Everybody was standing around the jukebox which was beginning to blast, "Rave On." The owner of the Arcade didn't allow anyone to actually dance so we all sort of just jiggled up and down; or at least the girls did while the boys beat on the slot machines looking for forgotten pennies. I leaned against a pinball machine while Jean went to the toilet. Two pinball machines up from me a group of boys was lounging and showing off. I was trying not to stare but one of them kept leaning forward and snapping his fingers at me. I started to blush and wished Jean would hurry up and come back. My heart sank, I could see she had stopped to talk to Connie and Rita.

I felt a flick of fingers on my arm. The boy who had been snapping his fingers was standing next to me. I crossed my arms tightly across my chest. My eyes were riveted on the jukebox. He was laughing softly and raised his right arm, placing his hand against the wall so that I was standing within the arch made by his body and the wall. I then realized he was looking down at me and not up. Interested, I turned to look at him as he pulled a comb out of his pocket with his left hand and slowly combed his thick, greasy hair. Tucking the comb back in his pocket he ran his fingers through the front of his hair and pulled it forward over his forehead. I couldn't breathe. I couldn't move. This was happening to me and Jean wasn't watching. I tried to tap my right foot to the music but it stubbornly refused to move. Then my foot moved like it had a life of its own and I lost my balance, grazing the boy's chest with my shoulder. He leaned forward and said, "What's your name, love?" I whispered, "Joan," and wondered if I should have volunteered my last name as well. I noticed Jean, Connie and Rita were all standing around the bathroom door looking in my direction and giggling. Jean was sort of waving at me in between collapsing on Connie's shoulder.

"Well," he said, "I'm Mick from Manchester, but I'm out at Poulton right now." I nodded like I'd know that, then hoped he wouldn't notice that I had.

"What are you doing next Saturday?" he asked. Taking a deep breath, and, as Mum says, the bull by the horns, I said back, "Seeing you?" He nodded and businesslike said, "Six o'clock outside the Arcade," and lowered his arm, tweaked my scarf, and sauntered back to his friends who were laughing and pushing at each other. I saw Jean coming towards me; Connie and Rita were gone, and she was sort of white around her nose. She could hardly open her teeth to talk. When she did she sort of hissed, "he's a Teddy boy, a Borstal boy. You're Mum'll kill you." She was pulling on my sweater. I shook her off. I needed to think. I had done it, well, almost. I was ready for initiation. If only I didn't have to wait an entire week. And what if he was joking? What if he didn't show up? Worse yet, what if I didn't show up?

I left Jean to catch the bus feeling like I had betrayed her. There was no-one home. I opened a can of baked beans, my all time favorite food, and dumped it into a pan. While I toasted some bread I got a plate and a fork. I was startled to see Rose's pearl necklace was still lying in the drawer. I put the toast on the plate and covered it with the hot beans. I ate it without chewing and washed it down with a glass of milk. It wasn't enough. I needed something more. I was foraging in the cupboards as Rose slipped through the back door. I touched my hands to my cheeks to feel if they were hot. Rose didn't seem to have noticed I was there. She sat down in my chair and twirled my empty plate around for what seemed like long minutes. I had forgotten to take off her scarf when I got home and I felt safer behind the open cupboard door. But Rose still didn't seem to notice me so I decided to brazen it out and sat down across from her. She was now peeling off her Tokay Rose nail polish and the flakes curled like torn rose petals on my plate. This was not like Rose to have been in the house for five minutes and not spot her clothes on me.

I was trying to decide whether to ask her to lend me money for fish and chips, when she leaned forward and rested her arms on the table. Her hands were palm down with fingers spread. She lifted her hands and was contemplating the damage to her nails intently as she said, "I'm pregnant." I felt the shock of her words ripple down from my brain. We sat still in the silence which followed her words. She seemed to recede from me and shrink in her chair. I felt like something was ended but I wasn't sure what. Even though I had known what Rose did with her boyfriends it had not seemed real. It was just part of a game and now Rose had spoiled it. I felt anger rising inside me. I shifted sideways in my chair to face away from Rose. It was growing dark. I wondered if I should touch Rose but then she pushed herself out of the chair, looked at me and said, "Don't start messing around with boys," and left the room.

I put my plate and fork in the sink and listened to Rose's footsteps overhead; then the house fell silent. I left the kitchen, closing the door softly behind me. I sank down on the back steps pulling my skirt over my knees. It was dark now and I could barely see the pink of my socks. The silence was a pressure in my ears. I leaned my head against the side of the doorway and cried for Rose and for me.

TELL ME WHERE THE ROAD TURNS

CAROL ORLOCK

Jessica's skin was soft and smooth and still a little warm. Monica knew she should go before the sun left the high branches of the tulip tree. By then Jessica would be cool, no, cold. Jess did not breathe. She had not breathed for maybe an hour. Monica wished she knew a lullaby that said any of this in it.

The sheets were crumpled where Jessica had gripped them in one fist when they made love. Lovemaking today was gentle, unexceptional. Monica wondered idly, as she had wondered often over the last year or two, if this was how old married couples felt, lust building up over a week or so, the familiar haven of a lover's arms, and then the sweet acquaintance, the knowledge of how that skin would feel if she did this, or this, or this now. She supposed love grew even more intimate, more ordinary, from here on in. Then she remembered. Jessica lay dead beside her. She had died of a stroke. Their love would not grow more ordinary.

Monica had arrived at Jessica's small house at two. They planned a picnic out behind the abandoned army barracks off State Route 40. Of course there was danger in going anywhere together. There was danger they would be seen, danger they would be noticed, that anyone with a grudge, maybe the new nurse on Two West, would connect the dots and make a whisper that turned into a dishonorable discharge. They discussed it many times in the early years, turning the words over and over, handing them back and forth until they seemed like a stain, spread over each other each time they touched.

Dishonorable discharge. Jess would repeat it. The head nurse in gynecology dishonorably discharged. People would react, Jess always said, the way they did to a homosexual man caught working in a boy's school. People would make another horror story out of it.

For her own part, Monica did not care. If they threw her out, she would find a way to live elsewhere. The world should tolerate the differences. Maybe the world, Jess argued, but not the army.

And to Jess the army was everything. She was career army. The army was the world, the army and her family. She rose through the ranks straight and true, like her father hoped, and made head nurse two years ago.

He had looked so damn proud. And Mom couldn't figure it out, Jess said the first time they were alone together after her trip home. Monica smiled, and wondered if Jess's joy felt any less for the secret she kept back, the old news Jess had never told them about her life.

For Jess's sake they kept apart, working the same ward and keeping the cool distance of professionals. Some patients sensed it, the drugged or crazy ones down in emergency. Like that one they had to manage together, Jess holding him down while Monica pulled and fastened the restraints. He howled and struggled, a scared animal, while they worked as one body. Then he suddenly stopped. He looked from one to the other, dazed, because he felt it too, their love flowing back and forth and into him.

"You two aren't sisters, right?" He stared, lucid for a split second. He looked at their faces, the tall blond Jessica and shorter, black haired Monica. "I give up. You know something I don't." Then he went limp while they finished him.

Or maybe it was simple paranoia. Maybe no one suspected. Maybe all their caution, the codes for when they would meet in the coffee shop, the seeming to shop separately at the same store then go home together, the weeks apart, the loneliness too, maybe all paranoia. But it was a small base, supply and munitions, and everybody knew everyone. And they all knew the retired general who was proud of his daughter. So Monica kept the secret for Jess.

Today was the same. Jess met her at the door and hurried to get inside, shutting it. Jess stood tall and thin in her gold bathrobe, the sun streaming through the window and glinting red on her thick blond hair. Her week-old permanent looked frizzy.

"I thought we were doing a picnic," Monica asked. Jess's face looked drawn, her blue eyes nearly gray with shadows of tension. She pulled her robe close, turned and led the way to the kitchen.

"I heard they're planning something, maneuvers or something, along State 40."

"So a couple of nurses happen by on a picnic. What's wrong with that?" Monica helped herself to a teabag from the glass bowl by the sink, took a cup and poured water from the kettle steaming on the stove.

"But it's probably Burdick. He's got maneuvers next week. Remember Burdick who we saw with his wife at Mario's last Wednesday?"

Monica set her cup across from Jess's, which was lukewarm and half-filled, on the kitchen table. The lid of the honey pot was askew and she straightened it. "So?" she said, but did not press. She could tell Jess was suffering another headache. That was reason enough not to go and she wished it were the real reason Jess still wore her bathrobe, unwilling to get dressed and go.

"You have another headache." She reached and lifted Jess's bangs back from her forehead.

"It's better. I was dizzy earlier." She lowered her eyes and her hand covered Monica's. She seemed small, childlike even though she was older, forty-six next winter and Monica turning forty. "It's been off and on, a couple days."

Cardiovascular, the word whispered in Monica's mind. She pushed it back. "You got checked?"

"Taylor looked me over Tuesday. Says it's the flu and everybody calling in sick because of it. He figures flu and the tension of working half-staff."

"He got it yet?" Monica laughed lightly.

"No, but it starts with a headache."

Monica tangled her fingers into Jess's and pulled them down to curl together on the cool table. The sun beat through the orange curtains, a hot August afternoon and no picnic. The room was starting to heat up.

The headaches had come off and on for two weeks now. Jess looked pale and drawn mornings on the ward, then perked up in the afternoon if the headache passed. One day last week she said she felt dizzy and lay down in the nurses' lounge for a half hour before it passed. Monica wanted to go to her, hold her, make her go home, but that broke the rules. It would frighten Jess.

"Who cares about an old picnic," she said and Jess brightened. She reached for Monica's other hand and drew them both to her across the table, nudging the honey pot aside. "Besides, what time do you have duty tonight?"

"Seven," Jess said, "and I want to lay in bed with the sun coming in all afternoon."

Monica left her tea cooling on the kitchen table and followed Jess. They lay propped on the pillows for a long time, talking, stroking each other. These last few years, more and more, Monica could not be sure which she loved most, this lean, big and graceful woman, or their beautiful ordinariness together.

She loved the pillow her shoulder burrowed into because it was Jess's, loved the old flute Jess kept on the mantle and always dusted and never learned how to play, loved how her lips knew the chip on the edge of the cup that was hers in Jess's kitchen.

The first few years, when they argued and fought, meant less than this. They had taken a long time getting used to each other, beyond the curves and sensitivities in each other's bodies. That came easy enough because they wanted it badly. It was the silence that took longer, the drifting afternoons after childhood memories had been told, angry silences when Monica wanted to go out and Jess could not feel safe, the silence late one night when Jess had cried and cried and then lay on Monica's shoulder, shaking and finally still. They had argued the usual ground and Jess remained afraid.

Monica stroked the thick blond hair until Jess's head lifted. "Tell me," Jess said. "I want to know where the road turns."

"Look, you can say if you're sorry," Monica told her. "If you're sorry, then it's over, but you can say it. Say you made a mistake. Go back to men, or nobody. I should think I understand."

Jess's face was red from weeping, but shock drained the color away. She was not sorry, she could never feel sorry. They loved each other and that was fact. Plain and simple.

"I knew when we met, just the way I always knew the important stuff. Like about being a nurse. Like I knew I was army. But I knew the why of those things too. Not like this." Her shoulders loosened, sloping downward. "I'll never understand this."

Jess's big frame felt small then, no more weight than a child, and her voice was small with uncertainty. She whispered each word distinctly, "Just tell me where the road turns. I hurt, I need to know."

"The road we took into this? Or where we're going?"

Jess said she'd take either one, but Monica could not find an answer. Not that day, not in all the years since. Yet that day she stopped complaining about the secrecy. That day they began knowing how to keep silences, and the sweet secret routine began to weave, transparent beween them.

She looked up now. She loved the tulip tree, the sun leaving its leaves, the older leaves deep in the trees turning brown already. Monica shifted the blanket she had draped between herself and Jess and eased her head down on it. She heard no heartbeat, nothing. She did not expect one, yet the silence disturbed her. She would go soon. At seven the hospital would call because Jess did not show up. They would hear the phone ring, but the ringing would make no sound here. The phone lay beside the bed, the box twisted from the wall. Later they would send someone to look for Jessica.

They had made love gently, taking their time. The sun glistened on Jess's pale skin. Monica held her, then felt herself tumble backward and Jessica's lips on her skin. They dawdled and enjoyed, playing for time, and the lovemaking drifted to its finish, meandering through a pause into the knowledge that it was over for this time. They settled backward on the pillows, Jess's eyes closed, Monica watching the paisley pattern the sun made between the shadows of leaves on the blanket. She must have dozed, must have slept not to have heard sooner. Suddenly she awoke with the bed trembling. Jess's body was shaking it.

Jess's head jerked back, her hand gripped to her eyes. Her head, it was her head, and from her cries it must have hurt fiercely. Monica pushed her back on the pillows, gripped the fingers to pry them loose and see Jess's eyes, terror-filled, twitching suddenly back toward the top of her head. A seizure. Not enough blood to the brain. Monica gripped her, held her head still so that its shaking did not hit the shelf at the head of the bed. She pummelled through the covers, hanging on to Jess's skull as the neck spasmed and bounced. Her other hand reached for the phone by the bed, punching buttons, but the receiver dropped clattering to the floor. She reached for it and felt Jess heave under her. She heard a voice on the line before it went dead. Jess's fist held the cord, falling backward again as the colored, electrical lines strained from the wall and broke.

For an instant Monica saw Jess's eyes. They opened slightly, like a child's last fight against sleep. They were clear and blue and seemed to plead for understanding. Even as she saw, Monica slid from the bed and was halfway into a step to the door. She was nude, she realized then, and understood what Jess meant, stooping back to sweep the gold robe from the side of the bed, pulling it over her. They would know why she was there. Dishonorable. She ran down the hall and pulled the front door open and almost ran from the porch before she realized her stupidity. The odds were ninety-nine to one against Jess surviving now. Minutes had passed, eight, ten, maybe twelve. Blood had been cut to the brain. One way in, one way out. Ninety-nine to one that Jess wouldn't make it, and with that look Jess asked to throw away the one.

Monica closed the front door and leaned against it, her pulse roaring in her ears. Then she made herself turn and go back. She checked the vital signs slowly, methodically, as she had been taught. They had both been right. When she was done she let the hard part of her mind go loose, let her arms circle Jess's waist, put her head into her belly and cried into the soft skin there.

Sunlight still came through the window, but the patterns of the leaves blurred away into shadows. It was time to go. Monica pulled the covers aside and smoothed her imprint from the sheet. They would think Jessica had tried to reach the phone. They would think she was alone. They must think that. Anger rose in her throat, the bitter taste of black tea. She pushed it down. It was Jessica's one chance in ninety-nine. She had chosen to throw it away.

Monica rinsed her cup in the sink and set it upside down on the drainboard. She wished she could take it with her, then decided she would. She carried it back to the bathroom where her clothes lay tangled on the floor.

The mirror reflected her body as she dressed. She thought of how Jess must have watched herself in this mirror. It had reflected them both younger. It probably saw the night they celebrated Jess's fortieth. Now it would not see either of them age or gain weight or go through menopause.

She walked slowly through the house to make sure nothing of hers remained. The cup rattled in her handbag as she opened the front door.

Jessica's key stood in the deadbolt lock. It had to be used to close the door from outside, but she had planned that when she lay beside her, loving her. It was dark now and she fitted the key by touch. The lock clicked and slowly, for silence, she lifted the frame of the window and reached in to the small table where Jessica's purse lay. She dropped the key inside and pushed the window closed.

THE CULTURAL WORKER

SUSAN DORO

The poem waited for her outside the wheel shop door. Waited, as if it were one of the leaning train wheels stacked against each other, like round brown five hundred pound dominoes. Train wheels waiting to be hauled inside the factory, machined to order, then mounted on shiny steel axles and rolled out the door into the Menomonee Valley train yard.

So too, the poem waited. It had been waiting for her to finish work since 3:30 that afternoon. Now it was midnight. Soon she would step out of second shift into the dark of the going home night.

Hours ago in the early evening, the summer sun hung low and rosy over old freight cars in the yard. The poem had gone to the window nearest the machine the woman was operating that night. The poem thought that the sunset would surely get her attention. But not tonight. She was measuring a train axle with a micrometer, straining on her tip toes to reach around its diameter. The poem could see she was too busy to be thinking poem words, so it did what it knew how to do.

It waited. Measuring minutes against the sun's shadows on the dirty cream colored brick wall. It waited, as 5 o'clock break time came. It waited and watched through a different window as the woman ate half of her sandwich sitting at the lunch table by the men's locker room, sharing a newspaper and talking with some of the guys. She was the only woman in the shop. There used to be two others but they got laid off. Now she was the only one of her kind left, and sometimes she was lonely. But tonight the poem saw that she was having a good time, joking with her "buddies."

It was an hour and a half later when the poem looked in again. The woman was standing with the micrometer in her hand, listening to a short elderly man with gray brown whiskers. He wore a work-worn green hard hat, low over his eyes. His hands glistened with dark brown dirty train bearing grease. In one, he held a red handled putty scraper. In the other, by their cuffs, a pair of oily rubber gloves. The ring finger was missing on that hand. A cigarette bobbed up and down from his mouth as he talked. Its ashes dusting the man's brown shirt every so often. The poem could catch only a few of the man's words. . ."wife. . .divorce. . .still love her. . .the kids don't. . ." The woman was intent on listening to the man. The poem went back to wait at the door until dinner break.

In summer it was still light at 8 in the evening, and the poem knew that the woman would come outside to sit on the long bench against the building. Most of the men would go out for dinner to the tavern up the hill, so she would usually be alone. Sometimes she would take a walk by the railroad tracks, heading under the freeway. There was a river to watch and listen to, and wild flowers to pick. In the early spring, there were little green onions and asparagus hidden in the tall grasses.

Sometimes she would read or write in her journal. But tonight she had no pad of paper, no pencil or pen. She was sitting on the bench, but she was leaning forward a bit, holding a book. A union agreement. And she was not alone. She and some other workers were talking words like "lost jobs . . . bankruptcy . . . lay offs beginning in July . . . the company can't . . . illegal . . . they'll try . . . four guys fired . . ." The poem saw it was useless to try to get into her head. Then the factory whistle blew and a foreman appeared in the doorway, motioning the woman and the men back to work.

The poem stayed outside.

At 10 o'clock the poem went to look in the window by the woman again. She was staring out into the blackness of the night, but she didn't notice the poem. Her eyes were taking in the silhouettes of axles and wheels and oil drums. Watching black birds fly in front of the huge pink street lights on tall poles that illuminated the train yard. Her face was feeling a good west wind blowing in. She wasn't thinking poem thoughts. She was thinking of going home and wishing the night would hurry so she could get there. "A few more axles," is what she was thinking, as she turned away from the warm starry night. A night smelling of Menomonee Valley city wilderness, and NOT the stockyards, thanks to the west wind. Away from the window she turned. Away from the poem looking in the window, and back to her job.

And finally it was midnight. The moon was high over the factory roof. The yard was a water colored wash of moonlight and pink from the lights in the valley. The moon was a white ball with a golden ring. The poem waited with the moon, holding its breath. The pink lights shone down over the top of the building, casting shadows on the path next to the tracks.

The woman would be the first ready to leave. Usually she waited for the guys by the little gray door at the far end of the shop. But tonight she had told them she was in a hurry. She stepped alone into the night as the midnight whistle blew. She was short, but her shadow was ten feet tall. She carried a paper sack of dirty work clothes in her arms. The poem was with her like her shadow, walking quickly. The farther away from the building, the taller her shadow grew, from the pink lights and the moon on her shoulders. Little rocks and pebbles at her feet crunched under her shoes. Each pebble had its own shadow, like pink moon rocks under her feet. She smiled to herself, enjoying the moment.

A cat meowed, and scampered under a parked freight car. Night birds called. Now her shadow split in two, growing taller, taller, taller. Catching pink lights on more poles in the train yard. She stepped carefully across one, two, three sets of tracks. Past stacks of unmachined main axles and rows of wheels. Past lines of mounted wheels and axles waiting to be shipped out. A lone black bird cawed at her from a telephone wire. Something stirred in her brain. Some disjointed words seemed to come together. She laughed aloud, and the crow cawed again, leaving its perch to fly over her head into the blackness beyond the realm of pink lights. Then suddenly the woman threw her head back and yelled up into the pink and black sky. "HEY. . . I'm a midnight rider. A cat's eye glider. I'm a second shift lady goin' home!"

She laughed again. And surprised and delighted, the poem jumped INSIDE HER like a fetus kicking in the ninth month. She hurried along, faster now, almost running the last few yards past the guard shanty.

She was at her car in the parking lot now. She unlocked its door, opened it and flung her sack of dirty clothes in the back seat. Getting in, she started the car up and aimed it out of the lot, waving to other workers that were now crossing the tracks behind her. Finally she would have time for herself. She felt the uneasy urgency she'd had all night, go from her in a deep earth moving sigh, as she drove past the guard shanty and turned up the road to the ramp leading from the valley.

And a poem was born, comfortable as a well fitting work shoe, and satisfying as the end of the work day. The poem. The woman. The machinist. All became one. And she sang to the hum of her car:

I'm a midnight rider
A cat's eye glider
I'm a second shift woman goin' home

I'm a moon rock walker
A night bird stalker
I'm a short tall shadow headin' home

I'm a cool old river
A seasoned survivor
I'm a factory workin' poet goin' home

COMMENCEMENT
KENYATTA KOONTZ

It's hot on this bus and my stomach is eating itself. Earlier I had been standing in the rain and liking it. My hair was so full of water that each new drop which landed pushed a stream down onto my face and it had felt like my forehead was crying. Evidence of the early morning drizzle is now taking its form inside against the window. I am one of many with hot hands and foreheads pressed against the glass, trying to determine how close we are to our destination. We all unbutton our coats now, pulling scarves just slightly away from our necks. The rain comes easily to these parts. It makes the blood in the streets flow a little less red, clot a little less quickly. Mixed with rain, blood covers more ground.

There's a war coming. I say this to myself as though I can see a deep, dark shadow of uniforms advancing over the distant hills, but it is in fact a presence in me, a sense of uneasy, nervous fear issuing from people everywhere. Sometimes it's so strong that it seems to come in waves of pure smell: thick and smoky and stinging as if they had just washed their clothes in it.

This morning, however, smells more like a wet dog. And it needs a bath. *I* need a bath. Seven-thirty always comes as a surprise to me. After eight hours of dirty floors and mops and toilets, seven-thirty in the morning is simply amazing, regardless of the way both of us tend to smell.

Today I will climb into the hottest bath I can find and sleep until I can wake up as young as any child.

There have always been better jobs that I can imagine, cities to visit where rain comes only when you pray for it, intelligent people who bend closer to listen to me as we raise our coffee to our lips at the same time in silent recognition. Taking this bus, I am sure there is so much to do, and I know that it will be largely a matter of beginning.

For ten years I have been a mole in my underground job: working my nights, sleeping my days. In the morning I can hardly believe I still have eyes. Like walking down a steep hill, I am holding a part of myself back to maintain balance. I often wish I would let myself fall.

There is a woman at the University where I clean who arrives at her office before I leave each morning. She is tall and beautiful and very smart. When she talks she uses words you've never heard before, even though you've been using them all your life. I imagine her looking up from her desk one day and smiling back. I imagine her handing me a book she has just finished reading and she knows I would just love it. Because I am forty, too, and there's something about the way I look. We would meet for dinner the following week and discuss the unusual ending and I would say how much better it would be another way and she would agree. In time she would tell me about her husband or her cat. How much she loves them both but they just don't understand her work, and I'll nod. I know what she means. Soon we'll be involved in research together, bent over books or test tubes, disagreeing over one method, then equally excited about another. We'll be sharing disappointments and devastating news from home. We'll take turns chewing on each other's cramps, dissolving the raw pain before concentrating on the subtle aches. I will have all of her problems and none of my own.

When evening has come a part of me rests with the sun. It has been Friday since I stepped off the bus this morning and no sooner. In my bath I have let the water talk to the tiredness in me, and all day I have been aware of this ocean that wants to expand. If I leave this city where my job greets me each night with a chain, where my daughter makes her own life now and where I visit her weekly, hacksaw in hand that I may impart wisdom of free movement; if I pack tonight and flow right on out of here, would the world survive? Without me to pick up on Sunday nights, would the bus simply abandon its route and crawl back home? The morning paper would have to give some account of my unexpected flight, with bold headlines pronouncing the shock. I don't know how my flowers would handle it, but I can't be bothered by their growth any longer. I have too much of my own to encourage, and I have so rarely received the sun. I know that it will be largely a matter of beginning. I know, too, that my fear is no excuse for rooting these feet in the kitchen, no matter how warm or well lit I have made it. There would always be those chains waiting. I must walk on out of here.

It is night and I am frying eggs. This way I will not be hungry tomorrow, where there is so much to do.

SPRING WALK

DIANA RIVERS

Mona sits up and throws off the covers. Ty snatches them back, gripping them tightly up around her shoulders.

"Mona, what the hell are you doing? It's Saturday morning. Let me sleep, for chrissake."

"It's a beautiful day, Ty. I don't want to spend one more spring weekend in town. We talked about driving out to Culver County if it was nice today."

Mona jumps to her feet, stretching her arms toward the ceiling. The apartment is filled with morning light. Lazily, from one partly open eye, Ty watches the sunlight move in patterns across Mona's body. Mona nudges Ty in the side with her foot. "I want to go somewhere, somewhere up high so I can look out at the world. I want to climb to the very top and see spring. A few mangy trees struggling to put out a few sooty leaves—that's not enough." She shakes her head till her hair flies around her face. "I have to get away from this damn town—at least for a day."

Ty groans. She always feels defensive when Mona talks this way about town. It's as if Ty's responsible, as if they hadn't both agreed to stay. "Later," she says, pulling the covers tighter. "We'll go later,"

"It's already nine thirty. I've been trying to wake you up for half an hour. By the time we get there it will be noon." Mona slaps the wall hard with her hand. "Ty, are we going or not?" When she gets no response, she pries the covers out from under Ty's feet and pulls them sideways on the floor, leaving Ty curled naked on the bed.

Later, as they're driving south through the soft spring sunshine, Mona says, "I'd like to go up Cedar Hollow and climb to the top of those bluffs. There must be a way through."

Ty laughs. "The top of the bluffs, eh? Hell, why not? Everytime I see them from down below I want to be up there. This time we'll do it."

Ty is wide awake now. She's very glad to be out of town. She loves the curving country roads and drives too fast, tires squealing in the sharp bends. Her window is wide open making the car chilly, but she doesn't shut it. Farms roll away on either side and as always Ty tries to imagine how people manage to survive in the country. It's hard land. Rocks jut up through the new green of the pasture. Does it make people gentle, she wonders, to be living so close to the earth, or do they get hard fighting it? She tries to read the answer in the faces they pass, men driving old pickups with gun racks in the back. Mona cuts through her thoughts.

"I wonder if we should have called anyone. Maybe Jessica or Terry would have liked to come with us." Her voice is pulled away on the wind.

"I'm glad we didn't," Ty says decisively. "I'm glad it's just the two of us."

At the risk of their low town car, they park at the far end of an old logging road. When they get out, Ty straps on her hunting knife. Mona's amused. "I see you brought your weapon with you."

Ty grins and shrugs. "You never know what might happen back here in the woods. Besides I don't get to wear it in town."

The valley around them is filled with the fresh soft colors of buds, pale green and maroon and lime-yellow, like new fur growing up the hillside but the land is open, not yet overgrown. They can still see the shape of it, cut and molded by ancient floods.

Going up the valley they move slowly, looking at everything. Mona stops often to pick up little things. Ty is sharply aware of her, her animal-quick movements, her intentness, the pleasure with which she gathers things Ty wouldn't have noticed, a person so known and familiar to her and at the same time different, changed, much more herself in this setting. Glancing at Mona, Ty thinks: that woman is very precious to me. But Ty would never say it aloud. Instead, she asks, almost sharply, "Why are you picking up all that stuff? You'll have your pockets bulging before we get there."

Mona laughs and pats her pockets. "It's all light, little bits of this land, of this day. I'm going to make a necklace, string it together so it has meaning, ceremonial more than for wearing – a ceremonial spring necklace." She strokes Ty's face lightly with a blue jay feather, then slips it in her pocket. The deep, sharp blue flashes between them for a moment.

Ty stoops quickly and scoops up something from the dry leaves. "That's for your necklace, too," she says, setting a fragile snail shell in Mona's hand. Their eyes meet. They stand that way for a moment, bound by their eyes, their hands hardly touching.

"It's so silent," Mona says softly. "I feel as if we're all alone here, as if the woods are ours."

Ty nods. "I love the quiet. It calms me. I'm glad it's not fall when the hunters are out. It's not safe then to be a creature in the woods, not even a two-legged one."

Mona shivers. "Let's not talk about it. That's six months away. For now it's ours." She turns away from the creek and starts up the steep slope toward the bluff with Ty following. They're mostly silent, the climb taking all their energy. It's rough land, boulders and fallen trees. The last part – finding a pass through the bluff face and scrambling up – is a struggle that taxes their town selves. They push and pull each other in turn and finally haul themselves, laughing and panting, over the rim. After a moment to catch her breath, Mona jumps to her feet and raises her arms, shouting out at the dizzying space. Her voice echoes back to them from the hills.

Ty aches all over but feels victorious. For two years she's been looking up at that spot with longing, and now she's standing there. She slips her arm around Mona. "The very top," she whispers against Mona's ear. Under them the land sweeps away in a soft sea of spring green, swaying with the wind.

Mona makes a wide sweep with her hand. "I bet there's no one else in this whole valley, not another human being." They are standing on a stone terrace jutting out over the valley. From there they can see the hills curving past each other till they turn blue in the distance. In back of them big pines sigh in the wind and across the way a twin outcrop of rock reaches toward them over the chasm, the back of it dark with cedar trees. Patches of thick pale moss cover the stones at their feet.

Mona stretches out on the moss and Ty stretches out next to her. They lie there for a long while, touching along the whole length of their bodies, not speaking, each of them gazing hungrily, lovingly into the deep folds of the land below.

At last Mona says softly, "It's almost too much. . ."

"Why we live in town. . ." Ty mumbles and doesn't bother to finish her thought.

When Mona finally stands up to stretch, the wind is blowing harder. It makes her sway slightly on her feet. "Look! Over there!" She points toward the bluff across the valley. A flock of crows is rising and falling like waves through the top of the trees, silver when the sun hits them and then black when they turn, up and down, silver and black, over and over against the pale green. "So beautiful . . ." she whispers.

Wild and raucous, the sound of crows comes to them intermittently through the wind. Hearing them, Ty feels a catch in her heart – so much pleasure it's like a stab of pain. She sits up and wraps her arms around her knees. "Crows make me nostalgic. They take me back to when I was little and used to hang out in the woods behind my grandmother's. When I heard the crows my heart would ache, wanting to travel. Now when I hear them, my heart aches wanting to go back there."

"They make me want to fly," Mona goes over and stands at the very edge, rocking on the balls of her feet. ". . . to just spread my wings and soar out over that valley."

"Mona, get back from there," Ty says sharply. "The rocks are dangerous. They crumble. People get killed in these bluffs."

"Not me. I like to stand at the edge of things. It gives me a sense of freedom, of being alive."

"Mona, please!" Ty can feel the ache of fear at the back of her knees and up through the arches of her feet. The drop is hundreds of feet down a sheer bluff wall into a jumble of jagged rocks. "Mona!"

Mona steps back with a shrug of annoyance. Ty finds herself smiling and frowning at the same time. Mona's charming and irritating qualities are so closely entangled.

Stooping suddenly, Mona picks up something shiny and hands it to Ty. "What is it?"

Ty looks at it and hands it back, shaking her head. "The casing from a shell. Bird shot."

"They sit up here and shoot birds?" Mona sounds shocked and incredulous, and Ty feels that familiar tug of anger at Mona's innocence.

"Probably. Why not? It's a good place to see from." There's a bitter edge in Ty's voice, a combined anger at Mona and at the hunters.

"They shoot those crows?"

"And hawks and buzzards – anything that flies."

"Damn fools. If something moves, shoot it. If it's beautiful, kill it." Mona shakes her fist at an invisible enemy.

Ty shakes her head again. "If I live to be an old, old woman, I will never understand them. Why they take pleasure in that – never." She can't imagine sitting up there in that place, so high and beautiful and in a way sacred, though she wouldn't have used that word, and shooting at something higher and freer, shattering its flight and bringing it down ripped and bleeding out of the sky.

Mona comes to squat beside her, turning the shell over and over in her fingers. She shuts her eyes and tilts her head back, looking inward. "Sometimes when I hear hounds I think what it's like to be a raccoon trapped up a tree. I feel the fear. No place to go. The dogs are down below, leaping and barking and the hunters are coming with their guns."

After a long silence, Ty says slowly, "Once in the winter – I found a dead deer. She had dragged herself for a long way before she finally died. There was a wide red streak in the snow and all around the marks from her struggle."

Mona clears a small circle on the rock, brushing back the moss and leaves and twigs with her hands. She stands the spent shell up in the middle.

"Why don't you throw that away, Mona? It's ugly."

"No, it goes in the necklace. I don't know how yet, but it's part of this day like the feathers and the snail shell. It means something." She takes the other things out of her pockets. Sheltering them from the wind, she arranges them around the circle with the shell at the center: the blue jay feather and a cardinal feather and a soft barred feather that might have been from a hawk or an owl, three gleaming acorns, a hickory shell split with its double inner ear laid open, some grooved and sculpted seed heads and the fragile gray-white snail shell. "I won't know how they all go together till I get them home. But everything has meaning. It's all . . ."

Ty stands up suddenly. "I know – it all has cosmic significance. Let's go to the creek." She feels oppressed by Mona's airyness.

"Don't spoil things, Ty. I feel you getting moody."

"I just want to get to the creek while there's still some sun on it – ritual start of spring swim."

"It'll be too cold."

"You always say that and then you're the first one in." They both laugh and the tension eases. Mona gives Ty a quick hug. Then she gathers her treasures and fits them carefully in her breast pockets.

They start scrambling down with Ty in front. Part way, Mona stops to stare back at the bluff rising over them, red and orange, streaked with dark water lines. "Look at that," she shouts to Ty. "I didn't notice it on the way up." She's pointing to a narrow ledge that curves for a ways around the rock face. "It's just wide enough to climb on."

Ty turns back quickly. "Mona, for chrissake!"

But Mona is already crawling out. "I'll come right back, Ty. It's safe. I just have to try it." When she gets to the far end, she sits dangling her feet over the edge.

Looking up at her, so precariously balanced over that drop, so fragile and daring and foolish, Ty feels waves of love and anger coursing through her. "Mona, come back here."

"Ty, I'm fine. Stop fussing. Look – I've never fallen off anything yet."

It's true, Ty thinks, for all the crazy things she does, Mona never gets hurt. Sometimes it seems to Ty as if she's challenging the gods.

"It's beautiful out here," Mona calls to her. "Like an eagle's nest." Mona's voice has a seductive singing quality, the way it does in bed. "Why don't you come out with me, Ty?"

"Because I have sense enough to be afraid," Ty says quickly and then wonders if some of her annoyance isn't envy. How can Mona feel so magically impervious? Ty can't bear to look at her anymore. It's too frightening, but the picture is already burned into her brain – that tiny figure suspended against the vast red rock. "Look, you do whatever you're doing. I'm going to the creek." As she turns to start down again there's a loud sound.

"That sounds like a shot."

"Not likely, no hunters this time of year."

"But it could be someone doing target practice."

"Out here? Why would anyone do that out here?"

There's another sound, louder and closer this time, that's clearly a shot. The crows rise over the bluffs and wheel down the valley, cawing loudly. Mona shouts, "Hey, don't shoot. There are people over here." The shots seem to be coming across from the opposite bluff. "Ty, wait for me," she calls. "I'm coming down." Mona begins crawling back quickly. There's a third shot that hits the bluff above them, showering down rock fragments.

"Stop that, you damn fools!"

"Mona, shut up and get off there!" Ty yells at her. "They're really shooting at you."

"They can't be. That's crazy. They can see it's a person." But she's moving as fast as she can along the narrow lip of rock. There's a fourth and a fifth shot. Mona screams. Her body jerks. One leg is hanging off the edge at a strange angle. "I'm hit, I'm shot." She's scrabbling with her hands, trying to keep from toppling over.

"I'm coming, Mona. Hold on." Ty is crawling to her from the other side, heedless now of the drop below. "Grab my hand, I'll pull you back," she shouts. They lock hands. "Push with your other hand and foot." Their bodies scrape on the rough stone. It resists them, catching and snagging at their clothes, tearing their skin. There's one more shot that hits far off to the side, then Ty pulls them both off the low end of the ledge, falling back in the underbrush to cushion Mona's fall. After that there's a final scatter of shots, none of them close. Ty holds Mona tight against her, kissing her face. "Oh honey, honey, we have to get you somewhere and fix you up."

Mona's whole body is shaking. "Ty, they shot me. They shot me just like an animal out on that ledge." There's almost as much outrage in her voice as fear.

Ty tries to look past her. They – what they – she thinks, terrified. Where are they? Will they shoot again? She can't see anything up there, no motion, no clothes. The shot were coming from across the way, maybe from behind the cedar trees. She eases herself out from under Mona's body. "We have to get away from here right now. It's not safe." She's talking fast, trying to help Mona up. "Can you stand on that leg? Can you walk?"

Mona pulls herself upright, holding onto a sapling. Sweat breaks out on her face. She shakes her head. "I can't put any weight on it. I can't move."

"Then wrap your arms around my neck and hold on. We have to get around the corner to where the bluff will shelter us."

She's glad Mona's not heavy. Even so, it's incredibly hard. Fighting the underbrush and vines, Ty pulls herself from sapling to sapling, up against the steep incline with Mona clinging to her back.

"At least they've stopped shooting," Mona whispers against Ty's ear. Her voice is a dry rustle, barely audible. Ty doesn't say anything. She would have preferred more shots to silence. The grip Mona has on her neck is choking her. The only sounds now are her own staggering steps and Mona's jerky breathing. Mona's body is getting heavier as they go, as if she's losing consciousness. Ty wants to talk, to keep contact, but she doesn't have the strength. Each step is harder. She keeps seeing, over and over in her mind's eye, flashes of Mona sitting out at the end of the ledge.

The cut in the bluff face is almost like a small cave. Ty struggles inside and eases Mona down in the dirt. Quickly she takes off her jacket and covers Mona with it.

"We're safe here – at least for a while. Now I can deal with your leg." Ty leans over and Mona tries to pull away.

"It hurts. Keep away. Don't touch it." Mona's voice is high and strange with a crazy edge to it.

"I have to, Mona. I have to stop the bleeding." There's blood oozing through the pant leg into the dirt. Ty strips off her shirt and rips out the sleeves with the help of her knife. Forcing herself to control her shaking hands, she ties the two sleeves together for a tourniquet. Mona pulls at her hand, struggling weakly against her when she tries to get it into place. "Mona, please. I have to do this."

"It hurts, it hurts. Leave me alone."

When she's finished, Ty stands exhausted and trembling, leaning against the rock wall. Her hands are sticky with blood. She glances out. It's still the same soft spring green out there, as if nothing has happened – only the crows have gone. And the light has shifted. Not much daylight left. Not much time. Now, for the first time since the shooting started, Ty feels the full impact of it – the terror. Not one of their friends, no one in that whole town knows where they've gone. Would they ever be found? . . . ever? She has a momentary flash of newspaper headlines . . ." car found by . . ." and a picture of their bodies lying lumpy and distorted in the cave. Then she gives her head a shake. "Hold on, Ty," she tells herself harshly. "You can't afford to give way. Whatever needs to be done, you have to do it." Mona is too far gone to help. But when Ty tries to think about it, the way to the car seems unimaginably long, thousands of impossible steps. The car, the safe familiar car is parked in another country. Driving there together that morning seems to have happened some different year. Mona is reaching for her now and shouting with pain.

"Mona, you have to be quiet." Ty says it sharply but Mona doesn't respond. She's semi-conscious, moaning and tossing under Ty's jacket. Ty steps out past the entrance of the overhang and stands listening. From far away below her she can hear the steady sound of footsteps in the dry leaves. Quickly, deliberately, she gathers a pile of rocks from the debris around her. Then she steps back inside, puts one hand gently over Mona's mouth and with her knife in the other, squats down to wait.

DINORAH

RUTHANN ROBSON

I. PAYING DUES

There comes a time when a person and her story must separate, which is something I've had to learn to accept. A story needs to be told, though a person may think her story best forgotten. A person often believes her story belongs only to herself, but that is never true.

I am Dinorah's story. It is clear that she isn't going to tell me, she left me behind, for dead. So I must tell myself. If I tell on Dinorah as well, that is too bad. For I don't owe her anything.

It isn't that I don't like Dinorah, I do. Though I'll admit I've always thought her view of the world rather skewed. One version of me blames her mother, a woman round of eye and flesh, who refused to learn English and habitually committed herself to state hospitals for extreme treatments because she was "nervous." Of course she would be nervous, as the creator of a cauldron of five daughters boiling with the blood of the Carribean. Another version of me blames Dinorah's father, a bona fide traitor if ever there was one. He gave his life and breath to

Castro, then deserted Cuba after Castro was in power two years. The revolution was too successful, he said, casting doubt on Castro's sincerity and politics. So Papi brought his pregnant wife and two daughters to America where assimilation is his new revolution and he works at the Cuban Refugee Center.

America. Land of the neurotic and home of the envious. Dinorah was the first of the daughters to be born within its borders, cradled by its dissatisfactions. So great was the parents' joy at birthing an American citizen, they almost forgot to be disappointed she was not male.

She was a bright child. Smart as a boy, Papi said. Too bright, her aunts said. Her mother didn't say anything, spending most of her next two pregnancies in state hospitals.

Dinorah studied like mad.

Childhood passed.

She had a prayer, an ambition. It was a little poem she called "freedom." She wanted to be the author of her own story; it would be a grand novel full of garrets, passions, artists and beards. At eighteen, she moved to Paris.

At eighteen and a half, she came back to America, back to her parents' little stucco house in South Florida. She ate sour oranges from the tree she had watered as a child. She was predictably pregnant. She did the predictable thing for a dark haired Latin Catholic girl to do.

She went back to school; to nursing school.

Dinorah studied like mad.

The trauma of the abortion passed.

She recited a poem she entitled "escape." It was less lyrical than "freedom," but had a more insistent voice. She still wanted to write her own story.

When she graduated fourth from her nursing school class of two hundred and sixteen, having made at least a B in every subject except obstetrics, her family did not come to the ceremony. Her mother, resting in the little stucco house, said she was too tired to drive the ten miles to the college. Her father was swamped at the Refugee Center assisting Mariel Cubans toward assimilation. Her sisters were all married and pregnant.

I was a lonely story, but Dinorah refused to see me that way. She practiced being a heroine. She got a good job in the intensive care unit of a highly respected, lousy and holy hospital. She married a gringo intern. She divorced him. She tried to control me. She thought of her lost baby only when she drove home every morning at the end of her 11 to 7 shift. At her tiny Coconut Grove apartment, she often took a Valencia orange from the tree she shared with seven other tenants. Sometimes she would sit on the steps with one of the other tenants, a man named Craig, and offer him a section of orange. He always refused.

What Craig offered Dinorah, and what she did not refuse, was endless anecdotes about his two part-time jobs as a male dancer and a female impersonator. She laughed. They shared dinners and beers while the rest of the tenants were grumbling themselves from sleep to face the day. They began to share beds and private jokes and joints. They began to share some feeling that other characters in other stories might call love. They were a couple; a pair. They might even be described as outrageously striking. Dinorah's black thick hair tangled with Craig's reddish blond mane, cropped close to the head and billowing into a wild pony tail at the crown. They were both very tanned: Dinorah's skin the brown of chestnuts from Craig's New England childhood; Craig's skin the burnt sienna favored by a certain Parisienne artist whose face Dinorah had almost forgotten. Dinorah's eyes were deep and brown, her fingers long, her body lanky, except for the thighs which were thick as trunks of twenty year old citrus trees. Craig's eyes were speckled a soft blue, his body nearly hairless (Dinorah wondered if he shaved his chest and legs) and his shoulders widely curved. He liked to wear a brown corduroy shirt over a woman's tailored blouse made of aqua silk.

Dinorah, in her white uniform, came home from work one morning with a nauseous feeling tugging at her hem. When she saw the eviction notice tacked to Craig's door, she felt like she was rereading her own story. Him: gone. Her: pregnant.

A nurse should know better, but she hadn't. Or maybe she had. I watched her callously evaluating the evidence of Craig's gene pool before she consented to allow any part of his body to swim in her. But I cannot pretend to decipher what she really intended; what was accident and what was artifice. It is arrogance which makes a story attempt to fit the motivations of its characters into neat molds. I have had to learn to be humble.

I did, however, notice a cold imperative which settled in Dinorah's throat. It was not poetry or song, but had the music of an algebraic equation. It did not go to find Craig at the bar. It did not wait for Craig to call, but when he did, it relayed the message that she was quitting her job and moving north.

She tried to delude me that we were not going back to her parents' house, until we were in the narrow driveway and she could pretend no longer. She had loaded her Datsun past all recognized safety levels with useless possessions like wool sweaters and nursing school notebooks. In the same close kitchen in which she had told her father she had wrecked her bicycle, she told him she was fired from her job. Both times, she lied with an effortlessness that amazed me. Her younger sister had smashed the red bicycle in revenge fifteen years ago. Yesterday, she quit her job without notice.

Both Dinorah's deceits elicited protective sympathy from her father. He makes her flan, with extra caramel, just as he had done when she was a child. He swings into action, which for him means getting on the telephone. This time, he is not calling his best friend who owned a bicycle shop in Cuba. This time he is calling his best friend, a Guatemalan volunteer from the Amnesty Workgroup. Papi repeats his own name three times before it is apparently recognized and he is allowed to proceed with his inquiries about paying jobs for nurses. After a few more phone calls, Dinorah's qualifications land her an almost definite job at a maternity clinic for migrant farmworkers. The clinic is in a trailer ten miles west of Indiantown, Florida, otherwise known as out in the middle of nowhere. The job comes with a place for her to live, a trailer within walking distance. Perfect. They are desperate for nurses. She is desperate.

Her Papi is satisfied. He has rescued another soul in America. He kisses her at the place her cheekbone becomes her eye socket. I am dizzy from all the deception.

When Papi has gone to visit the state hospital, Dinorah finishes the pyrex pan of flan. She can always blame one of her sisters for her greed. She sits in the yard, waiting for one of them to appear, either pregnant or clutching babies or both. She is still alone when she vomits curdled custard on the exposed roots of the sour orange tree.

II. NURSING

The work at the maternity clinic is tiresome. The trailer is hot and crowded. Appointments are scheduled for the visiting doctor and the three nurses two days a week, from eight a.m. until seven p.m. Sometimes Dinorah sees over a hundred women in various stages of pregnancy and post partum recovery within forty-eight hours. The other three days are devoted to lab work, paper work and emergencies. Dinorah is the only medical person present at the delivery of seven babies. Unlike the visiting doctor, she does not claim all the credit for the miracle of birth.

Dinorah's own body blossoms. Except for her uniform, she could be mistaken for one of the patients. She never is.

I hum through the days. I have never felt so settled. I feel accepted, justified. I am traded with the stories of other women. I allow everything that is negative to be edited from me, including disapproval.

A stickler for accuracy, I would have bargained with Dinorah if she had wanted to rewrite Craig's departure as a divorce, or even a death. But she never asked, so how could I offer? When the visiting doctor recommended an abortion to the five months pregnant Dinorah, commenting that "what the world doesn't need is another brown bastard," and appealing to Dinorah to consider her career, she was unruffled. Even when we were alone in our rickety one bedroom trailer, Dinorah was serene. We were so close then, so close.

Three weeks before the baby is due, Dinorah is given a baby shower. The nurses give her blankets and booties and a book of baby names. The visiting doctor gives her a cheap plastic rattle. The social worker gives her a big yellow ball. One of her patients gives her a set of bibs with the day of the week printed on them. Dinorah cries. It was once expected that she would take some time off to wait for the birth of the baby, but no one has been hired to take her place and she says she feels fine. She continues to tend to other pregnant women, trading stories of false pains and water retention.

Three weeks after the baby was due, Dinorah is still tending to pregnant women and still pregnant herself. She has twice refused caesareans scheduled by the visiting doctor who thinks that the brown bastard's life is in danger. The clinic trailer rocks with Dinorah's defiance. The nurses continually recalculate Dinorah's due date on their little cardboard dials. The migrant women laugh and some shrug. Dinorah shrugs and laughs as well.

If Dinorah is scared, she doesn't let anyone know, not even me. She busies herself in the house trailer, making it ready for her child. She reads and rereads NAME YOUR BABY. She starts taking long walks through the groves at night and stealing the last of the ripened ruby orange, that seedy strain still cultivated for its ornamental bloody look. After her nightly hike, Dinorah drinks castor oil in a glass of white wine. She lights purple candles at midnight. Sometimes she even imagines telepathically sending my odd turn of events to Craig, somewhere in the world, a character in someone else's story by now, she supposes.

The night before El Dia de Candeleria, she drinks half a bottle of wine, a quarter of a cup of castor oil and a glass of pulpy ruby orange juice. She wills the baby to be born tomorrow. She will name the baby Bridget, patron saint of the day of candles and Irish, like Craig. She will name the baby Devin, for he would be a poet.

But the day comes and goes. The radio at the clinic reports that the groundhog has not seen its shadow. There will be more winter in some parts of the world. Near Indiantown, it is already hot. There has been no freeze this year; no damaged crops. The sweat pours from Dinorah as well as the migrant workers.

If the baby waits twelve more days, she can name him Valentine, or she can name her Valerie. The visiting doctor warns Dinorah that he will tie her down and slit her open before then – or take her to court. He does not seem to be joking.

It is the eighth day of the shortest month and Dinorah recognizes the searing start of labor, alone in her trailer. She is afraid to call the visiting doctor too early; afraid that he will slice her open merely for convenience or even to be spiteful. In less than fifteen minutes, she is not capable of envisioning alternatives. Her pain blinds her. The seven hundred yards to the maternity clinic might as well be seven hundred light years. She can hardly move – and all she wants to do is move. She is vomiting half an hour later when the baby's head crowns.

She looks at the clock and notes it is midnight as she cuts the cord, making two creatures from one. She counts fingers and toes, and massages her daughter. The baby is wrinkled and red and endowed with dark eyelashes, strawberry blonde hair, pale skin and slate eyes.

Dinorah tries to feed the baby, but she turns her head from her mother's breast and squeals. Dinorah is tired from birthing, as is the baby. They sleep on the bloody bed until morning.

Leafing through NAME YOUR BABY, Dinorah decides upon the name Alicia. It seems to fit the person who had flown from her body hours before. Dinorah likes it because it is not the name of her mother, or any of her sisters, or even her aunts. In fact, the only person she has ever known by that name was a classmate with blonde hair in the fifth grade. She did not recall the classmate or the name until it lifted itself out of the ten thousand other names for her baby nestled in the book. It attracts her because it is derived from Alice, which is derived from Altheia, which means truth. So, Dinorah discards the other nine thousand nine hundred and ninety nine names and settles on a derivation of truth.

Alicia, Alicia, she whispers, and with her professional hand she jams the baby's head against a breast huge as a pink balloon until the squawking baby squeezes her eyes so tight her face dissolves into a wrinkle and she finally starts to nurse.

III. THE HAPPY ENDING

I want to unburden myself about a thousand details about those first days when Alicia was making herself known as an indomitable character: how she spread her fingers wide; how her eyes were like tunnels into the unsparing Florida sky; how she would sniff for milk and allow herself to be persuaded each time to suckle. Like all stories, I collect snippets from life, scenes that my characters will call memories, and because they are remembered – or told – such events are clothed with meaning. One of the things I've learned from being Dinorah's story, however, is that not every act brims with significance. Those that do are often unnoticed.

So, what is important about the first few weeks of Alicia's life, at least from my perspective, is not when or whether Dinorah told her parents about Alicia, or whether Craig was missed or what Alicia wore. What is important is not how the nurses or the social worker or the patients fussed over Alicia. It is not even important that the visiting doctor commented to

Dinorah that Alicia was not as brown as he thought she would be, and how Dinorah laughed in reply that although that was true the child was still a bastard; and how the visiting doctor and the unwed mother seemed to be friends after that. What is important is a casual drifting from Dinorah's one bedroom trailer to the dingy clinic trailer.

I must confess, I was so interested in other things, like the sweet curve of Alicia's smallest toe, that I did not notice the monumental initial act. Perhaps it was another nurse who asked Dinorah to please hand her a chart, or a pen, or vitamins. Perhaps Dinorah merely reached for a rubber glove or the cardboard due date dial with her one free hand. Or perhaps it was the visiting doctor who asked Dinorah to assist because the baby was asleep anyway. This first act led to others, and to others.

By the time Alicia is two months old, she is firmly committed to a schedule that includes going to work every morning, participating in demonstrations of breastfeeding and taking a nap at precisely whatever time she feels like it. She is cradled and rocked by her mother, by the other nurses, by patients and even by the visiting doctor. She is charmed in several dialects of Spanish, in southern and northern accents of American English, in Creole and in Mesquite.

She grows, and people remark on her growth as if it were unusual, as if babies did not grow in the natural course of things. "I can't believe how she's grown," they say in happy amazement. Her abilities grow along with her body. She learns to roll over, to sit up, to crawl. When she stands up for the first time, she holds onto the metal leg of an examining table. Ten people applaud, including Dinorah, the visiting doctor, the social worker and the patient atop the table. When she learns to take steps, she uses the plastic chairs in the reception area to balance herself and maintain her position among the children of the waiting patients. Her eyes remain blue, her skin fair. Her knees become dimpled with strength. She starts to talk without words in a private language that Dinorah sometimes thinks only a mother can understand.

As well as going to work everyday with Dinorah, Alicia goes everywhere else that Dinorah does. They sleep together in the same second hand double bed and drink the same juice Dinorah squeezed from whatever oranges are in season. They go to the laundromat in Indiantown. They give lectures at the migrant camps on prenatal care and birth control. They attend a going away party for the social worker, who is leaving for Nicaragua.

They do not go to see Alicia's grandparents. After the birth, Papi had said he would send one of his best friends out to pick up Dinorah and the baby, but Dinorah refused. Papi swore at Dinorah through the labyrinth of telephone wires which connected the little stucco house to the maternity clinic trailer: "You think you don't need us!?!" It was Papi's ultimate accusation. He could forgive the bastard, but not independence.

Papi was right. Dinorah thinks she doesn't need her parents, or anyone, except Alicia. She feels rich with friends close enough to help her and cheer her, but not close enough to criticize. Everyone says she is a good mother, except her own mother, who sends no word from the state hospital. Dinorah is content without being stagnant; she feels capable without being rigid. Alicia is a laughing child who minds her mother without being servile. If either of them dream of Craig as a cavity in their perfect life, or of anyone else who might appear as a lack, they simply move a little closer to each other in their sleep and the dream dissolves.

I wish I could stop here, with the happy ending. But I am committed to accuracy.

It isn't that Dinorah was blithely trodding the grassy path between the clinic trailer and her trailer, mindlessly picking up oranges. It isn't that Dinorah didn't shift Alicia from hip to hip always expecting to spot the tragedy that would rend them apart. Dinorah knew that happiness is always temporary.

It isn't that I, always the pessimist, didn't expect something to happen. If someone had given me a choice, I know I would have abandoned Dinorah and Alicia at this moment.

IV. THE TRIAL

Conflicting stories are vying for space in the small courtroom. I can hardly breathe.

The judge looks like he is choking in his too tight collar; his face is red above his white shirt and black robe. He appears alternately bored and smug. He holds the only pen in the courtroom; his signature at the bottom of an order can change people's lives.

The jury box is empty. Dinorah is not facing jail time and is not entitled to a jury. She has not been charged with a crime; that would be easier to defend. It would have also given her the right to be provided with an attorney.

She stands alone behind one of the two small tables which face the judge. Alone and without Alicia.

At the other table stands Susan Anderson, or as she prefers to be called, Miss Anderson. Her shoulder length brown hair is caught neatly back with a rubber band covered by an ironed white ribbon. She wears a navy blue dress trimmed in white twill and white pumps. She spent forty minutes putting on her make-up that morning to achieve a natural look. She is unmistakably white.

Dinorah is suddenly something other than white; something less than white. She knew she should not appear in court in a white uniform or a pair of jeans, but that was all she had, except for the roach eaten paisley nylon dress that now collects her sweat. She had bitten her nails down to the quick. Her only jewelry is a man's Timex purchased for its prominent second hand sweep. She wishes she would have worn her uniform. Wouldn't that have made her look more professional? – or only more brown?

The judge instructs them to be seated.

Miss Anderson, the new social worker, starts her speech. She recites that two days ago she filed a petition to have Alicia declared a dependent child and that she recommends that custody of the child be placed with the state. She blandly explains her action by her conclusion that the child is neglected, deprived, and subject to great psychological danger.

The judge asks Dinorah if she understood, as if he doubts she can understand English, or any language. She did, she says, but her voice rushes on: Couldn't she have time to hire a lawyer? Couldn't she have time to get witnesses? She had only received the notice of the hearing yesterday.

The judge mumbles some numbers that apparently represent a state law that, he explains, requires that this hearing occur within seventy-two hours after a social worker has filed a petition. He tells Miss Anderson to proceed.

Miss Anderson is happy to comply. She begins to retell me in terms of unhealthy psychological dependency. She recasts me as her own story, which always lingers over one specific moment during her childhood on the Florida Panhandle. She had skipped home one sixth grade afternoon, her pointed glasses slipping down her sweaty nose, excited about telling her mother that she had won the citizenship award. Her mother berated her: Susan should have won the scholarship award as well. Good citizenship wouldn't get her into college.

But it had. And now a judge is listening to what she has to say:

The child has slept in the same bed as the mother since birth, inhibiting psychological independence.

The judge does not listen to Dinorah's silent defenses:

She's only a baby.

There is the possibility of lesbian interaction.

What is she talking about? Babies are sensual, not sexual.

The child has not yet had even her first set of DPT shots.

She doesn't need them if she's still nursing. Besides; four babies died last year of allergic reactions.

The child is still breastfeeding, which is unnatural at her advanced age.

Unnatural? The advanced age of fourteen months?

The child's mother's own mother has been in and out of state mental hospitals for the last fifteen years.

How does she know that?

The child has no father.

Most kids don't.

The child lives isolated in a one bedroom trailer.

We both live there.

The child is taken to a dirty clinic everyday and exposed to infection.

I'm a nurse, goddamn it, and I work there.

The child has no opportunity to interact with others in her own age range.

The patients have children and Alicia plays with them.

The child has no schedule.

How can you call a kid that gets to work every morning at seven a.m. a kid without a schedule?

The child was observed with a bruise on her forehead.

She runs! She runs and falls.

Miss Anderson then attempts to evoke Alicia for the court's benefit. The social worker's Alicia is blonde and blue eyed and destined for severe psychological trauma if she is not removed from Dinorah's dark influences. Alicia is horribly unhappy, forced into an unsuitable environment. Alicia is a child who cries for no reason and is afraid of strangers.

The Alicia described by Miss Anderson the social worker, based upon her three observations of the child, is not Dinorah's Alicia. That child was taken from her this morning as she appeared in the courtroom as directed. Dinorah had felt as if she was being analyzed in her reaction as she let go of the child's hand. Did she show enough feeling? Not enough? She wanted to scream as Alicia did, with unabated and ignorant agony. She wanted to allow the tears to swell her face and redden her eyes.

Dinorah remains silent and stubborn. I see her face tighten into the mask of the migrant mothers when the visiting doctor tells them to spread their legs and put their puffy feet into the metal stirrups. There is no one in the courtroom to pat Dinorah's arm; to say "squeeze my hand if it hurts," as Dinorah had so often done for the expectant mothers.

Dinorah is alone in a government room inartfully paneled by the lowest private bidder. Dinorah is alone because she is a mother, the only mother present. Miss Anderson is not a mother and does not have any desire to be. She thinks children should be raised only by the emotionally mature. She also thinks that only the emotionally immature attempt to fill their needs by having children. The judge is not a mother either, though he has performed some acts which have made him a father. He considers himself devoted to his offspring, though he will admit that he considers children little better than animals until they are articulate in the same language in which he is.

When Miss Anderson finally ends telling the story which she hopes the judge will believe is me, the judge asks Dinorah if she has anything to say. I am ready; ready to tell about love, to tell about self sufficiency, to tell about true devotion. I have never been so ready to steal a show in my entire life.

But Dinorah forgets me. She forgets all her accomplishments. She forgets all the wonderful things we have done together and the witty ways I have of recounting our adventures. She forgets how she cut Alicia's umbilical cord.She forgets her methodical morning ritual of straining even the seediest parson brown or ruby red oranges and holding the juice up to the light before she pours it into a spill proof cup for Alicia at six a.m.

Dinorah feels that her own memory, her own language, has abandoned her. She has been overcome by a monotone of English which seeks to be neutral. She is suffocating in words that come from books and not from life; words that represent concepts and not things that have smells. She cannot speak. She looks at the judge, so pale, so deadly white, and she chokes with Alicia's tears. She makes no sounds.

I want to shake her, but a story does not have arms, only words. I am screaming and she cannot hear me.

She hears the judge, his voice smooth as huge stones carved with commandments. He renders his judgment. There isn't enough to put the child in a state shelter, he says, although there is enough to make him believe that some state supervision is required. He pronounces "a few conditions" that will govern the life of Dinorah and Alicia:

1. That the child be placed in a state licensed child care facility while the mother is at work and that the child shall not be taken to her mother's place of employment.

2. That suitable housing with at least two bedrooms be obtained and that the child shall have her own bed.

3. That the child shall be given all vaccinations and immunizations immediately.

4. That the mother attend parenting classes.

5. That the home shall be visited by a social worker on a weekly basis.

The judge asks Dinorah if she understands. She does. A few conditions. She could do anything if it meant having Alicia. A few conditions. The court would review the situation in six months. A few conditions.

V. THE EXECUTION OF JUDGMENT

Although the clinic trailer is packed with children and women like beautiful mangoes in various stages of ripening, it is barren without Alicia. The nurses miss her. The patients ask about her. The visiting doctor longs for her to come and hug his pant leg while he is trying to do something much more important. Dinorah is always looking for her, then remembering with a sigh of resignation.

Alicia is screaming her way through the day at Le Petit Academy, a franchise in Indiantown that has agreed to warehouse another child for a mere $75 a week. Miss Anderson's office is a half a mile away and she stops by the only state licensed child care facility within thirty miles to ensure that Alicia is in attendance. She watches the child, alone in a playpen, and is informed that the child has been screaming nonstop for five hours. Miss Anderson is confident that it is for Alicia's own good, in the long run. At least she won't grow up to be a lesbian or a drug addict.

Dinorah's breasts are swollen hard and huge, itching with milk that seeps from them like sticky tears. She goes to the bathroom to squeeze them and to cry. She cannot look at her patients' children. She watches the clock. The day lasts forever.

When she picks up Alicia from Le Petit Academy, the sky almost dark, Alicia clutches her mother's uniform. Dinorah notices the white powder over Alicia's eyes and smells the talc. Alicia laughs in high pitched squeals. Dinorah decides not to tell them not to use talc on Alicia. Dinorah has always thought talc dangerous for babies' sensitive skin, but she wants to be cooperative. Alicia is happy to be in the car, across from her mother, buckled into the seat. The child falls asleep and Dinorah sings with the radio.

In their little trailer, Dinorah removes the soaked diaper from Alicia. Alicia has never had a rash, which Dinorah attributes to her use of cornstarch rather than talcum powder. She notices blotches on Alicia's smooth thigh.

Then she notices a perfectly round burn on Alicia's leg.

She tries to put the color red out of her mind. She will be sensible. She thinks of the black of the judge's robes.

She takes a bath with her baby. In the tub, Alicia sucks wildly, Dinorah's breast humming with relief and her other breast jealously spewing wasted milk. The child falls asleep and Dinorah finishes bathing her and washing her hair.

There is a knock on the door. Dinorah does not answer.

The second hand crib, procured by the visiting doctor, sits in the only bedroom. Tomorrow, Dinorah will look for a larger house, one with two bedrooms. It is time the child had a room of her own, she thinks, the judge is right. She rocks the already sleeping baby in the oak rocking chair which also sits in the bedroom, but Dinorah is disappointed that Alicia remains asleep. She remembers the nights she would sigh with relief that the seemingly endlessly energetic child had given herself over to sleep. But now, there is so little time to be together. She puts Alicia in her new bed with its miniature mattress and perfectly painted white bars.

There is another knock on the metal door. Again, Dinorah does not answer. She falls asleep laying diagonally across the bed that once belonged to herself and someone else.

When she hears Alicia's cry, it sounds far away. Dinorah remembers the crib. In half sleep, she takes the baby to her breast and back into the bed. Dinorah swears to herself that when Alicia gets back to sleep, she will put her back into the crib.

Dinorah wakes up, the trailer still clotted with darkness, knowing that something is wrong. Alicia is gone from the cradle of her arm. Perhaps she put her back in the crib and does not remember, but the crib is empty.

Dinorah can hear Alicia's whining cry as she turns on the light. She looks under the covers, but the baby is not in the bed. The baby is under the bed, an extension cord draped across her neck.

Dinorah turns pale; paler than Miss Susan Anderson; paler than the judge.

This is the first time Alicia has ever tumbled from the bed. This is the first time Dinorah has ever slept through Alicia's slightest disturbance. This is the first time Dinorah has ever felt careless, negligent, scared. This is the first time Dinorah has ever looked at Alicia and seen a stranger.

Mother and daughter have been separated into two distinct creatures. What has been killed is their instinct for interdependency; their instinct for mutual survival.

It was my intention to have their connections atrophy naturally, like the way a tree bears a white blossom and nurtures it into a heavy fruit which it allows to drop from its branches. Then the tree has the pleasure of admiring a lush orangeness on the ground and the fruit has the joy of viewing the blue of the sky framed by branches to which it is not attached.

Things, however, are not turning out as I planned. I am finding it harder and harder to reach Dinorah. She rarely remembers me, even as she rocks Alicia until dawn with my rhythm. Alicia sleeps peacefully, oblivious to the judgment of the court which occupies her mother's mind and confident that tomorrow will be like all the rest of the days before yesterday.

VI. THE ENDING

This is as far as I can go; as far as my tale can extend. I do know that Dinorah and Alicia left town and that they went further than Indiantown, for I looked for them there. They left me behind, because they did not trust me not to give them away. I do not want to believe that they wanted no part of me.

So, I stay around here. I never go to visit Papi or the state mental hospital. I am resurrected at the clinic during dull paperwork. I am related in Spanish and English and Mesquite. Someone tells me to the former social worker, who has returned from Nicaragua. The visiting doctor tries to revamp me and include something about him being in love with Dinorah. Miss Anderson tries to distort me into a morality lesson for the needy. The judge only digests enough of me to close his file.

I wander the groves, alone. I describe the blood that stripes the flesh of the succulent ruby oranges for my own amusement. I no longer expect that Dinorah and Alicia will come back for me. I am learning to accept the fact that Dinorah has abandoned me, as she has always abandoned everything except Alicia.

Still, I like to imagine her somewhere warm, her brown skin tanned and glowing. I like to imagine Alicia growing and growing and watering trees. I like to think that Dinorah and Alicia are enjoying their happy ending – at least temporarily.

LESSONS
SUSAN B. STRONG

Karen Fernandez was standing in front of her tenth grade Chemistry class speaking to them about Alkaline Earth Metals. She was pleased with this class. It was late October, still fairly early in the first semester, and she had devoted her lectures so far to describing the basic structure of atoms and molecules, chemical bonds. Now she was moving them on, explaining the periodic table, energy levels, showing them how to use what they knew about a chemical's atomic structure to predict how it would react.

It's such an elegant theory, she thought, knowing they would not have to discuss the messy exceptions to the rules until much later in the year. By then, they would be comfortable enough with the logic to find the exceptions interesting.

"If an atom will try to attain the electronic structure of the Nobel Gas closest to it in the periodic table," she paused to make sure they were still with her, "what will the Alkaline Earth Metals do?"

A shy boy named Bill looked up hopefully. "Lose two electrons?" he offered.

"Yes, and what are the ways for, say magnesium, to lose two electrons?"

"It could form a bond with something that needed to gain two," said a red-haired girl in the front row.

"Very good," Karen said, then showed them how to figure out which elements would tend to give up electrons and which would tend to acquire them. Soon they were pairing up atoms, like and unlike, matching chemical needs. For homework, she gave them a list of atoms to react, in the proper proportions, and they dispersed with the energy of youth.

Karen erased the chalkboard, carefully gathered up her notes and zippered them in her briefcase. She locked up her room then walked across the parklike campus to the teacher's lounge/lunchroom. Several students greeted her as she walked. Her slight, athletic build, wavy black hair, her attractive young-looking face didn't stand out from the crowds of students. It probably also helped that she didn't have the aloofness so many of her colleagues did, not feeling any need for it.

She could sense her students' respect for her by the way they responded in her classes. She was very clear about what she expected from them: to take responsibility for their own learning and to learn to think. Maybe a lot to ask of a group of adolescents and some of the kids seemed disappointed that she wouldn't spoon feed them. But there were always a few bright ones; these she could spark, and she used their questions to help keep the class interest warm. She felt like she was finally beginning to hit her stride as a teacher. She had been hired right out of college, six years ago. Now she was tenured, getting it a year early, in recognition of her skills.

There were only four teachers remaining in the lounge when Mike Flanagan hurried in at quarter to one. Karen, Steve Walters, Jim Brown, and Susan Shafer were sitting at a table in the corner joking about the mudslinging in the campaigns for next week's mayoral election. A hotly contested election was a rarity in Roseville. A town of about 30,000 people, its comfortable existence was supported primarily by the large woolen mills. Its houses were tidy clapboard, its streets tree-lined. A fair proportion of its residents went to college; the more adventurous didn't come home, moving on to Buffalo or New York City or other places more receptive to new ideas than Roseville.

Flanagan's face was flushed and his thick eyebrows looked moist. He was a heavy man, with a shiny head and a fatherly face. Karen felt his pale blue eyes looking worriedly at her then moving to the door.

"Is something wrong, Mike?"

"I need to see you in my office right away," he answered, looking embarrassed as the other teachers all glanced at Karen.

"Sure, Mike,' she said, smiling queasily and trying to decode the message on his face.

He closed the door to his office, a first as far as Karen could remember. He was an open and able administrator, Karen had been pleased to discover. She had not expected such competence at a small town high school. They had worked closely together a year ago fighting a book banning effort by a bible-toting member of the School Board.

"I got a call from Missy Harrison this morning," Flanagan said, rubbing his forehead as if he was trying to erase the call from his mind.

"What's her problem? She knows we've got her beat on those books."

"It's not the books this time," he said. "I'm afraid it could be even messier. She's getting a little too personal, and you seem to be the subject of her attentions."

Karen's stomach started an unpleasant churning as she felt Flanagan's eyes on her face, then on her body. She had always managed to keep her private life separate from her teaching, never dreaming of any problems.

"Oh?" she said at last.

"She demanded that I fire you," Flanagan said reluctantly.

Karen stopped breathing for a minute. "What??"

"Moral Turpitude." He rolled his eyes at the ceiling.

"Oh, come on Mike, what is going on?"

He curled up his nose like a pig and reproduced the whining sound of Missy Harrison's voice. "She informed me that you engage in 'unnatural sex acts with women.' That you are a 'danger to our impressionable youth. And must be removed at once.'"

"Oh, Christ. Is this a bad dream or what? Where does she get this? Her kids have never even been in my classes. They probably aren't bright enough."

"Karen, I told her the whole thing is ridiculous. I won't have her trying to bully my staff."

Karen sighed. "Wonderful. What was her response?"

"Oh, she started into her 'If you know what's good for you' routine."

Karen smiled at his shiny head.

"The worst of it is," he went on, "is that even though she doesn't have a leg to stand on, she's apparently planning on filling the town paper with all sorts of dirt."

Karen sighed and found herself twisting her long hair. "Why is she doing this?"

"I don't know. She's probably still mad about losing the book showdown. But you aren't the only teacher on that committee."

Karen glanced at the window just as a particularly vicious gust of wind tore off most of the autumn leaves remaining on a large maple.

"Karen, I know you live out in the country, Stoughton Road, yes?"

"Yes, Mike."

"Well. . . what exactly is the situation out there? I mean, I know you're not married. . . and I've never heard you mention any boyfriends."

Karen snorted. "I'm a chemistry teacher, and as far as I know, a damn good one. My personal life is none of anybody's business. Not some old prude on the School Board, and not yours either, Mike."

Flanagan caressed his heavy eyebrows for a couple of minutes. "So you are. . . one of them," he said quietly.

"That's not what I said."

"Well, it's going to be awfully hard to defend you if I can't deny her charges."

Karen glared at him. Her olive-skinned face had turned a fiery copper. She noticed that Flanagan was starting to look sick.

"All right, all right," he said finally. "I guess there's not much more I can do for now. Maybe it will blow over. Or maybe she'll lose her taste for blood."

Karen wasn't sure how she got through her afternoon classes. Her mind kept going back to those days when she first started teaching, fresh out of college, newly in love. Although she never said a word about Sarah she thought for sure everyone knew. Sarah, Sarah, Sarah. Karen felt her presence in the classroom, in the car, on the walk across campus. She heard her voice in the wind, the chirping birds, the chattering students. But if anyone noticed that she was flying a little high, their teasing didn't get too personal. When she moved in with Sarah, they thought it made perfect sense for a young single teacher to share a house with another woman. It was a lovely old house, halfway between Roseville, where Karen taught, and Buffalo, where Sarah worked. As the years passed, it became home, they became family, Sarah's children became her children.

Sarah Friedman tidied up her desk at the public defender's office, bid her colleagues good day, and departed. It was Friday afternoon and one of those rare weekends when she wasn't bringing any work home with her. She hoped Karen would have something tasty cooking when she got home.

Sarah pulled into the driveway and spotted Karen sitting on the front porch. She was wearing baggy jeans and a heavy sweater, and had her feet on the railing, a beer in her hand. She was staring off into the woods, almost dark now in the fading light. She must have had one of those days, Sarah thought as she climbed up the steps and kissed her on the cheek. Leaves were blowing all around, some skittering across the large old country porch. Sarah could hear her two daughters playing in the back yard, their giggles mixing with little barks from the new puppy.

"What's the good news?"

Karen stood up and shook her head sourly. "You'll never believe this one."

"Try me."

They went inside and warmed up the house with a large crackling fire. Karen reluctantly related her conversation in the principal's office. Sarah couldn't believe it. Like she couldn't believe it when she'd lived in the city – and came home one day to find her house had been robbed. Someone smashed a window and came in through her bedroom. The entire house was ransacked. Her dresser was dumped on the floor, her desk trashed, her valuables gone. For that she had insurance, to replace the goods at least, if not the illusion of security. But who would compensate Karen for her stolen career?

Karen had gone into the kitchen and was tending a pot of spaghetti while trying to convince the girls to finish making a salad. At seven and eight, Jessica and Lisa were easily distracted, especially with a puppy in the house. Karen wondered what to tell them, how they would take it if things got rough with the School Board. Karen hated the thought of the girls being dragged into it. They were so sweet and trusting. They would be teased unmercifully by the other kids at school. She remembered how kids often parroted their families' prejudices, with that untempered meanness that children sometimes have. Maybe she should just quit and spare them all the grief.

After dinner, they sent the girls upstairs, and decided not to tell them anything until there was a chance that they'd hear about it anyway. Karen and Sarah spent most of the weekend venting their outrage and plotting strategies. By Sunday night they had come up with a plan. Karen would deny nothing, but admit nothing. Since it was clear that she was an exemplary teacher, and the accusations did not involve her interactions with students but were purely an attack on her personal life, she would stand behind her right to privacy.

They felt like they knew the School Board fairly well, based on last year's book banning fight. The Board members were basically a timid lot, except for the vindictive Missy Harrison. They weren't really interested in breaking new ground and had voted against banning certain books primarily because Mike Flanagan and the other principals were so strongly opposed. In this case, the School District did have a policy against hiring "known homosexuals" but Karen and Sarah figured they had a chance; if Flanagan would back them up on the privacy issue, the Board might go along with it.

Monday morning, Karen walked into class with a feeling of doom in her heart. She was trying, and it was a serious effort, to keep it off her face. Her students didn't appear to notice. They were soon into a discussion on the subtleties of covalent and ionic bonding. Karen felt some of the tension draining from her body as the day passed with a deceptive routineness. She didn't see Mike Flanagan at all. On the drive home that afternoon, she began to nurture a possibility, a vague hope that she could still be a teacher.

The rest of the week also passed uneventfully, if stressfully. That weekend, Karen and Sarah packed up the kids and drove up to the mountains to a friend's ski cabin. From that snowy paradise, Roseville High School seemed like another world.

The following Thursday afternoon Flanagan got another call from Missy Harrison. She made the same demands as before but this time when Mike told her to drop it, she asked him why his wife had divorced him three years ago. And how many weekend fishing trips he had taken with the geometry teacher. Then she laid her ultimatum on him: he had until Monday to get rid of Karen. If he didn't, it would be on the agenda for the next School Board meeting.

Sure enough, there was a nasty little article in Monday night's paper. Karen's anger flared again. What right had these two-bit bigots to attack her for something they knew nothing about? Since she'd met Sarah she was finally happy, she finally felt good – after a childhood of putdowns, too bright for her own good, and an adolescence of pretending, knowing she was different.

The next morning at school she expected teenage snickering. But they were too shocked to snicker, these kids she'd been prodding to think, to question.

"What's it to the School Board?" they asked. "Are you really gay?/Do they think you'll corrupt us?/Do they think its contagious?/What's the big deal?/Maybe they're jealous?" They didn't talk much about chemistry that morning. A few of the kids were very quiet. Three boys and two girls announced that they would be at the meeting to support her.

The other teachers she was close to were also shaken up, feeling this blast of ill-will as an omen for all of them. Karen was grateful for their support. She could have done without the attention, however, as she squirmed and fidgeted, feeling a little like a yeast on a microscope slide, with that giant eye above watching to see whether the stain will take.

In the two weeks before the School Board hearing Flanagan was deluged with calls from outraged citizens. Some insisted that he must support his teachers, that quality was the bottom line. Others demanded that he fire the troublemaker, as if Karen was the one who had caused the trouble. One particularly forward caller reminded him of official School District policy on the issue and threatened to have him fired if he recommended otherwise. That one really hit him where it hurt. At forty-five, he told Karen, he wasn't planning on looking for another job.

"I have too much invested in this school to get booted out now."

"Don't you think I do, as well?"

"I'll do my best," he said lamely, "but it's not up to me to challenge district policy."

"Mike, if you let them do this to me the other teachers won't give you the time of day."

"I know," he said. "I know."

The meeting room at Roseville High School was filled to capacity. The storm windows were already up for the winter, precluding anyone's letting a bit of fresh air into the room. All nine members of the School Board sat facing the crowd, at a long rectangular table at the front of the room. Near their table was a speaker's podium with a microphone. In the front row of about twenty rows of folding metal chairs sat Mike Flanagan, Karen Fernandez, Sarah Friedman, and four of Karen's fellow teachers from the high school.

Several of her students were in the hallway, outside the closed door, having been refused admittance by the Board. They were taking turns observing through a six by fourteen inch glass panel in the door. They were also muttering obscenities at the Board members, who claimed to be so concerned with their learning yet had locked them out of this hearing, which even from the hallway could be profoundly educational.

Missy Harrison opened the meeting, standing at the microphone in a gray wool suit, its hemline safely covering her knees. She droned on with a series of items until people were squirming in their seats, longing for a little breeze. Then she proceeded to condemn Karen Fernandez as unfit to be in a classroom, a danger to the tender minds of children.

Karen had steeled herself for days, anticipating this venom which Missy Harrison tried to disguise as decency. Still, she felt the poisonous words ripping into her. I wasn't born to be a martyr, she pleaded with herself and with whatever greater power might hear her.

Flanagan took the microphone when Mrs. Harrison was finished. He praised Karen's teaching, her methods, her commitment, her concern for her students. When he was asked specifically about the issue in question, he said it shouldn't be an issue.

"Karen has taught at Roseville for six years. I've seen her work wonders with some of our most worrisome students. Her private life is not a concern to me. I don't even know if she has a relationship of the kind you find so deplorable."

So far, so good, Karen thought.

"Mr. Flanagan," Missy Harrison hissed, "it is of great concern to this School Board and to this community whether we have allowed a deviant to be with our children. It had better be a concern of yours as well. Do you have a recommendation in this case?"

Mike extracted a handkerchief from his coat pocket and wiped his forehead. He looked at Karen, at Sarah, at the teachers from his school. He appeared to be stalling for time, hoping for some way out.

A sharp voice came from the long table. "Mr. Flanagan, there are other people waiting who would like to speak."

Mike cleared his throat. "As I said before . . . Karen is an excellent teacher. I don't think we need to worry about her . . . uh, behavior . . . affecting any students in a negative way. And I don't think dismissing one of our best teachers is a good idea."

"That's right!" someone yelled from the back of the room, then it seemed like everyone was shouting at once.

"She's a good teacher and we need her!"

"We need more good teachers, not less!"

"Not if they're queer!"

"Oh, come on, this is the twentieth century. The Puritans are dead!"

The little groups of people Karen had noticed when she first came in were reasserting themselves, though their strident voices intermingled. She hadn't known the strength of their feelings, the huge split in the town.

"We've got to protect our morals!"

"I don't want my children exposed to that woman!"

"What's the matter, you afraid they'll get some ideas?"

"Quiet please!" Missy Harrison demanded. "This is supposed to be a School Board meeting not a shouting match."

Mike was still standing at the microphone and he looked a bit startled when Mrs. Harrison turned sharply to him.

"Mr. Flanagan, are you aware of our School Board policy on this issue?"

"Yes," he said. "I know what the policy is."

"And are you aware that it is your job as principal of Roseville High School to administer according to the policies set forth by this School Board?"

"Yes," he said slowly.

"Keep that in mind as you give us your official recommendation on this issue."

"I have already told you my feelings on the matter, Mrs. Harrison." He brought out his handkerchief and dabbed his face again. Karen grabbed Sarah's hand. "However, it appears that as Principal of Roseville High . . . that I have no choice . . . but to go along with the motion for dismissal."

Karen shuddered in disbelief as he sat down. Coward, she thought, watching him shrink in his chair. He really thinks he can save himself by throwing me over? She wanted to scream at him and shake him, can't you see what you've done? But he looked so miserable and her anger was so numbing that she didn't do anything. She barely heard the parents who gave testimony, speaking of their children's progress in her classroom, of their appreciation for her style, her taking them seriously, how she taught them the logic not just the words. She barely heard Bill Williams talk about his son, about how Karen kept him from quitting school when he had one foot already out the door. She definitely didn't hear the two parents who pleaded with the Board to protect their children from this secret menace who had deceived them for six years.

Just before Karen was asked to the microphone she found herself moving forward in time, looking back on this night. She wasn't sure of the details but she felt a strength, survival, an expanding horizon. She found herself somewhere else, where the narrow minded folk would stand open-mouthed and silent. A new treatment for cancer, a safe disposal for nuclear waste, a breakthrough in architecture. Her future stretched before her. It was not a ruined future.

As she stepped to the front of the room she remembered the strategy she and Sarah had planned. It wouldn't save her now and she wasn't sure she wanted it to. Missy Harrison, instigator of the charges, had no questions. The other members of the Board hesitantly began.

"Ms. Fernandez, what effect do you think your behavior will have on your students?"

"Mr. Smith, I teach chemistry. The only behavior I have discussed with my students is chemical behavior, atoms, molecules, acids, and bases."

"Yes, but now that they know about your, uh. . . shall we say personal behavior?"

"The only reason they do is because the School Board has made it an issue. I don't see why it should be a problem, however. I'm more worried about the effects of this inquisition on their impressionable young minds. I've been trying to teach them to think for themselves, to make their own decisions." She looked over at the Board members, searching for any understanding of what she was trying to say. Not finding any on their faces, she went on. "If they have to worry about straying from the party line, you aren't going to see much creative thinking."

She was getting wound up trying to break through to these people. They seemed like such a complacent bunch; there wasn't any shouting coming from the long table. She wasn't sure if they would spend the energy to really consider her position. And if they would, could they even imagine what she felt like? Would it be safe to put themselves, for a brief theoretical moment, in her shoes?

Mr. Smith spoke up. "They are a bit young for creative thinking, Ms. Fernandez. Perhaps we had better get to the heart of this issue. We all know, by now, that district policy forbids employing teachers who are . . . uh, deviant. Is there any reason that we don't know about, Ms. Fernandez, that you should not be terminated from Roseville High School?"

"Would you like me to promise to be a good girl? Would you like me to deny that I love a woman? Do you want me to plead for mercy and say that it's all a big mistake and I'm sorry, it will never happen again, just let me keep my humble job at dear old Roseville?"

"If you were sincere," Missy Harrison said with glee in her voice, "we would consider it."

Sarah tried to catch Karen's eye and calm her down, but she was beyond that, beyond caring about pettiness and fear and ignorance.

"Well, I won't," she said calmly. "I care too much about these students to cave in to intimidation. I've been trying too hard to teach them to look for the truth. If the will of this School Board is a mandate for hypocrisy then I'm afraid you have much more of a problem than I do."

"Ms. Fernandez, this is your last chance. Is there any reason you should not be dismissed?"

"Yes," she replied. "I'm an excellent teacher, as you heard from Mr. Flanagan and the concerned parents."

"I'm afraid that is not the issue," Mr. Smith said.

"It should be!" shouted one of the parents.

"The issue is protecting our children from undesirables," Missy Harrison said angrily. "And I think we've had enough discussion."

The vote was five to four against Karen. She was the first one out of the door and she didn't know what to say to the students waiting in the hallway. Sarah joined her as Mike Flanagan slid by. The School Board emerged next, not looking at the students who joined hands and hissed.

ASHES

MARIAN MICHENER

While it was a strange solution to an even stranger problem, it was a good thing in the end my sister Jill was there. Because I never would have thought of it. For one thing, I hadn't slept since I'd heard about the wreck. When I thought about Blue and Carol, I'd get that dizzy feeling like when I ponder infinity too much, or what's beyond the edges of the universe, or where do chemicals come from. Grief is so obsessive I almost think it's the inverse of sex, the adrenaline rush of separation. It sharpens your senses. But it makes it impossible to sleep.

So I had a routine of lying still and letting myself sink just under the night surface for as long as I could. And every time the stunned feeling began to subside, I'd shiver back up again because I was afraid if I fell asleep, I'd wake up believing it.

The hardest thing was Carol being gone without my having one last chance to touch her. So, while I was lying tangled in my sheets, I'd close my eyes and make myself see her wearing those gray striped overalls with the dusty butt because she would sit anywhere in them. I'd contemplate the smile lines around her mouth. And those green eyes that would wink at me and bring me in. And I'd see her holding both my hands. But I couldn't feel the warmth that used to stream through her hands and set me humming. And I couldn't hold her there long enough to make her see that I couldn't stand to lose her. Eventually, I'd give up and tuck up that wisp of red hair that was eternally falling in her eyes.

And I'd tell myself she's ashes now. And I'd tell myself that's impossible. And I tell myself I could begin to accept it if I could have touched her one more time.

After I'd checked the green digits on the clock all night, it would finally be five, the earliest I could get out of bed without admitting I was going crazy. And I'd drink a pot of coffee and push dull-eyed into a schedule of things I thought I had to do, like reading the morning news one word at a time with an uncomprehending sense of responsibility, or posting numbers on clean ledger lines as if making them all add up helped. I'd stretch each task into the next until the sun was down and the dishes were washed and dried and stacked. Because, when I'd done everything I had to do, it would be time to wrestle with sleep again.

So by Saturday evening there was a fog buzzing in my ears as I drove my sister Jill up to the house in the woods. I wasn't giving in to the soothing lines of brush and trees along the county road. And where usually I would smile at the green tin number tacked to a creosoted post, instead I sympathized with the groan of the Volkswagen engine gearing down to climb the muddy driveway.

And there was Jill, stretching out the long family legs, looking like a funhouse reflection of me. She was lithe where I was haggard. And you wouldn't know the soft brown hair brushed down her back was the same basic stuff as my businesslike butch. My face felt as thin as her face looked to me. But hers had everything pushed upward: mouth, nose, cheekbones, eyebrows. I suppose it's what my face would have been if I'd been born the baby, squeezed out, squeezed in, spoiled and a little stuck up.

Not that I'm not glad my sister looks after herself. I haven't had to worry about her. And mostly I admire her being a woman who gets what she wants. But I was nervous bringing a stranger to the woods at a time like that. Jill hadn't known Blue and Carol. She's not a dyke. And I didn't think she was going to understand our sense of family.

As I tried to explain, it struck me as funny, how my friends and lovers call ourselves sisters and it means we mean to be intimate for life. But with Jill it means we always wind up facing the difference and distance that balance out being given to each other from the first.

She gave me this unconscious tolerant smile that irritated me in an old familiar way. I noticed the sweatshirt and jeans she'd put on, how they almost parodied my own clothes. And I remembered that she usually fits in all too well. Sometimes she seems spineless or chameleon to me that way. But sometimes I like her capacity to translate different worlds. She can go a lot of places. Which turns out to have advantages I hadn't begun to imagine. I knew she'd do okay at the land. And I was glad she was with me. Because I was beginning to fear that there wasn't time to put off being together. And because I've always trusted her caring when I've ached like I was aching then.

Walking into the sooty oak panelled livingroom was like walking underwater. If it hadn't been for the crackling from the potbelly stove, I would have thought the whole scene was behind glass. I had expected we'd all put our arms around each other. But I must have missed that moment because there was a standoff going on among the three women already there. I knew what it was about because there was nothing left to fight about except Carol's ashes.

Leah sat like a beaten bear in the center of the bald gray sofa. Her elbows rested on her knees. Her head and hands and breasts hung down. She looked defeated and unbudging at the same time. Her lips were firmly drawn over what she thought was her secret. She had loved Blue and never told her. She only ever let herself speak it though hard work. I'd seen it so many times, Blue proposing a project and then Leah sending her suggestions dancing along. Like when they decided to do a vegetarian pit roast for Blue and Carol's midsummer picnic this year. That's how Blue and Leah embraced, through their ideas in the charged air between them. It was as if bodies were too slow and earthbound to express their connection.

Leah had some kind of ethic about Blue and Carol's relationship, I guess. Or maybe she saw it as an organism, a piece of ground that nourished the good stuff she admired in Blue. And she cared for Carol, too. You just can't separate these things. I don't suppose there's a lesbian among us who hasn't had that camelot feeling. For Leah's part, she was stubborn and silent with her love. And even now, when none of us could reach them to hurt or help, she was still protecting Blue and Carol.

Leah's loss was the opposite that mirrored and doubled mine. I thought if I really touched her, the combined weight of her loss and mine would explode demanding to know: how could they leave us when we loved them so much? But she was wound so far inside her spiral shell I could afford to slip onto the couch next to her. Jill made like a bookend on the other side, a little too confident when even those of us who belonged there were so confused. As the sofa swelled to harbor all three of us, Jill reached her spidery, manicured hand around to touch my elbow. She gave me a dopey sort of pat like when we were kids and I knew damn well she had no idea what was bothering me so how could she act like she was so sure it was going to be okay? But even if I couldn't let myself feel her reaching, I understood it, and it helped.

I looked at Nancy, suspended midsentence in the rocker beside the stove. In a brown and green tweed jacket, she looked as tiny and neat as my grandmother's handwriting. All her power was focused on her steepled fingertips as if the next word might appear there. She was the lawyer who wrote Blue's will, so she knew, as usual, how things ought to go.

I think maybe Nancy feels about the law a lot like I feel about bookkeeping. Hardly anyone else understands how beautiful it can be when everything justifies, like all the pool-balls falling into the right pockets. And how, after you've taken pleasure in that for a lifetime, there comes a point when you see the whole elegant system crumbling in the face of meaninglessness. And you're embarrassed to have loved the structure so much. By then it's all you really know.

What Nancy finally said was, "If Carol had left me any word at all, I could have brought her home."

She shrugged and I could see extending from her outturned palms a spherical shape describing the limits of her skill. And how much lies wordless beyond that. She said, "I tried to make the parents understand."

"It's not that they don't." Vic sat on the floor, a lanky, muscular, sunburned woman with her arms wrapped around her knees. If the worn peartree pattern on the carpet under her could have borne fruit, it would have been Vic with her girl face and gardener's hands. She was the adopted relative in Blue and Carol's house. They liked to tell the story of how she hitchhiked into their lives on a desert highway one day. And stayed. In a role you wouldn't call spouse or sister or daughter exactly, but which was no less real for the lack of a name.

Blue's will made Vic caretaker of the house in the woods, holding it in trust for the community. I remembered how Vic had come, not so long ago, reminding us all of our own first legendary rush of feeling for women's land—room to shout, dance and weed the garden naked in the sun. How it had taken her longer than anyone else to understand that women could hurt each other here too. I had goosebumps for what Vic still stood to lose. Just for a moment, fear threatened to take the floorboards out from under me. Maybe there was no such thing as a community. What if it was just a figment of Blue and Carol's imagination? An illusion they had persuaded us of that we couldn't sustain without them.

But there was Vic believing all the harder for being left holding it. The room darkened. Nobody moved to turn on lights. Vic rubbed her curly blonde head and said, "We were close with her parents. At the hospital. They know how we feel. As far as they can. And they feel how they feel. And legally, like Nancy says, Carol is theirs."

Nancy leaned forward and rested her head on her fingertips. She waited.

And it was Leah who sank into the cushions of the couch and spit it out. "Men's law," she said. "How else could she wind up belonging to someone else even after she's gone?"

And I had to agree. Leah pushed herself up off the sofa and walked out to the porch with a purposeful gait she uses when she doesn't want to be bothered with anything but the task at hand.

I looked after her out the open door and wondered why Carol hadn't written a will. Of course, she never did think much about things beyond their immediate use. And the land was in Blue's name, which seemed odd because I always thought of it belonging to Carol – or Carol belonging to the land. She was the one who brought it alive for me, opened me up to my own relationship with it. And I think that was true for the others too. Even Blue. But Carol never did care to sort things out. Like how she wouldn't weed the garden because she swore she couldn't tell what belonged there and what didn't. It all looked like good eager tender green life to Carol.

But I did remember how, one day last Spring, we had all discussed without foreboding what we would want done with our things. Blue and Carol had been there and Leah and I and the truck farm collective that's since dispersed except for Vic. It had been part of arranging to be together for a long time. We had each spoken of our important things: one woman's flute, another's dog, poetry, tools. Right down to the ashes. And it had been Carol who had said, "Where else but the woods?" And we had all agreed. And I had almost felt tiny roots reaching down into what would be left of my heart when I was through with it. And Blue had stood there with her feet planted wide where the dust beat up out of the peartree carpet wearing a grin that was undaunted by such a long view. And she had said, "We'll be together," meaning, we had understood, not just all of us, but also her and Carol.

When Leah walked back in with an armload of wood and began stuffing it into the stove, I could see in the firelight that flickered around the shape of her long denim skirt how perfect her love had been. Who else would there ever be for the woman everyone leaned on but an outlaw like Blue with a glint in her eye that said: forget all that. Because Blue had a way of looking at you like she was going to fold her arms and wait until you got around to taking your own back. Just because she'd like to see it. What else would ever speak to Leah so dearly?

I wasn't completely surprised when Leah stayed crouched there, staring at the flames, and sighed and let Blue go one more time, just like she always had. She turned to face us and said, "We should ask Carol's parents to take Blue with them too."

Nancy shook her head without looking up.

Leah insisted. "We know they wanted to be here. We also know they wanted to be together. If they can only have one – who's to decide?"

This "who's to decide" neatly divides Nancy and Leah on every issue. None of us wanted to fight in that house on that night. But Nancy, being Nancy, had to say, "Blue's will directs us to scatter her ashes on the land. There is nothing for us to decide."

Even I wanted to say, that's just an accident, you know, what happened to get written down. And Leah couldn't fail to respond, "Dammit, Nancy, there's more than one law and you know it."

Vic picked up Leah's anger like a ball of yarn the cat's knocked over and wound it back up. She said, "You know, the way they were together was – related – to the place and the rest of us. I wouldn't feel right. Sending Blue away. And anyway, it would hurt too much."

Leah pounded her fists against her thighs until she found something else to do with her hands. She picked up a sleeping bag, wrapped it around her shoulders, disappeared through the kitchen and banged the back door.

Out of the corner of my eye, I saw Jill at the far end of the couch, the long hair along her curved back like a parenthesis at the edge of a sentence that wanted to form among us all. I couldn't catch her eye or break the silence to say to her, please understand how difficult this is.

But I left her in the room that was swirling into storm-clouds around Vic's lower lip because I wanted to catch Nancy, who had stood and dusted her knees and said, "I'll bring Blue's ashes tomorrow."

I fell into step behind her going out the door and walked with her down the driveway. In the wet forest smell of the night, the hug she gave me was bony and dry. I knew she would delay returning until just before the memorial to avoid further discussion.

The peace recovered from the crash of Nancy's car door and the scrape of her engine. One cold star broke through the mist. And I was left alone and wondering what it is that makes a body so alive it can hardly hold it in, like the pulse that used to dance in the soft spot where Carol's throat met her shoulders. And where does it go?

"What do you think happens when you die?' It was Jill's voice I heard as I stepped onto the porch. Sometimes I want to shut that girl up with her dumb impossible questions. She was sitting on the floor inside with one leg stretched out and her chin on one knee looking into Vic's round open face. I think I'm the only one in the world who ever suspects Jill of being ingratiating. In this case, I underestimated her.

I stopped and watched through the fine mesh of the screen door. Vic chewed on something, probably peppermint, and balanced her head forward on that strong neck. She said, "Nothing. I think this is it."

Jill said, "Me too."

Somehow it reminded me of when we were kids and my grandfather had died and I had dared Jill to touch the urn his ashes were in. I had been too scared. But she had done it. Flipping her hair off her face as if it had been a trifle.

To Vic she said slowly, "So what does it matter where the ashes are?"

Vic leaned back with a sad smile and chewed on that one. I don't know what she remembered while I remembered Carol pouring boiling water over the pennyroyal in the jade green teapot, Blue carving turkey with an artist's eye appreciating the table full of dyke christmas orphans.

Vic said, "It's hard. Going on and doing what we were going to do together – without them. If we had the ashes, it would feel a little easier."

Jill stood and stepped to the woodstove and I must admit I wanted to shake her. I wanted to say: Listen, Sis, if you're going to look into this woman's eyes as if you understood her dreams, you better understand. But there was a warning in the way she stood there with her back to me. Like when we were kids and she was up to some kind of scheme. It was beyond me what that could possibly lead to in this case. But I found myself smiling and shaking my head. Jill put a log on the fire. And Vic said gently, "We don't really need anymore fire."

And I felt a satisfying chill when I heard Jill say, "*I* do."

I stepped back into the woods and followed more the sensation than the sound of the creek down the hill in the damp darkness. The pines surrounding the cabin were shadows. But I kept remembering how they had quivered in the bright sunshine, the longest day of the year, when I had been there for the midsummer picnic. That had been a very green time. There had been more different and intense greens than ever before. You may think this was love, but I tell you it was color.

That day after the feasting had made us high and sleepy, Carol and I had escaped to the lean-to by the stream. She had showed me how to listen to the waves of silence in the water. It had been the first time I had seen the underflicker of light among the leaves. We had stretched out and watched the alder branch shadows moving on the water.

We were never lovers exactly. And maybe you'll think I don't have very good sex if I tell you that lying close and looking at the clouds unravelling in the sky with her was better than making love. But I do. And it was. I never told her outright that I was in love with her. But she had only to see how my eyes would have liked to swallow her whole. I think she knew.

That day she had asked me what part of the stream I felt most like. And I had picked out a peaceful pool banked with clover. I had hoped it looked as inviting as I felt. But she had surprised me, pointing for herself to the deep rush at the center downstream from where we lay. A part of the stream that was too deep to reach and long gone before I could see what it was. I had buried my head in the pillow of her shoulder with my heart breaking knowing I could never close the distance. She would always be running downstream from me. Even now. And I guess that's as close as I ever came to saying goodbye.

Later, when we had returned to the remains of the picnic in front of the farmhouse that day, Blue had only smiled at our unabashed blushes. But it was Leah who had glared at us and bustled tightly around the yard as if she didn't know what else to do. She had only let herself mutter through her teeth, "Let's clean up some of this trash."

I stopped trying to remember all the details, who said what, who stood where, who touched whom. I still had the funeral to face and I didn't need to spend the night collecting evidence. I found myself walking down the hill toward the alder stand and I realized I wasn't afraid of Leah anymore. I wanted to tell her we're all just trash anyway. Which made me laugh, if painfully. And hell, I was angry too. With whatever it is that swallowed our friends up and ripped a hole in our lives. I went ahead and threw a tantrum, stamping along the pine needle path. The earth just absorbed it all.

When I got to the lean-to someone was already there. It was Leah, huddled on her side as if she were sharing secrets with the dry patch of dirt deep in the shelter. The night was as wet and cold as it was going to get. I couldn't see anyplace better to be than eased down beside this woman listening for whatever she was finding there. I wanted to tell her I had a feeling Carol was coming home. That there's no place in the universe she can go that's farther than our love can reach.

I didn't exactly explode when I finally touched Leah. But I did fall apart and fall into myself and fall asleep against her back. The sound of the creek water ran together with the way my heart broke open in the night and I woke up so full of sadness I had to reach out and hold Leah warm against my wounded chest. And we rocked each other in stillness for a long time.

And my knees still shook when we walked back up through the woods. I tried to make the greenness shine there like it had before. It was autumn now anyway. I squinted at the red and orange leaves. But I knew that wasn't going to bring Carol back. As we got to the driveway, I gave up and closed my eyes. And when I opened them I could see fallen leaves moving on the breath of the wind. But I could also see my car was missing.

Jill was gone too. Which was typical. All morning I pretended not to be nervous about not knowing what was going on. My ears filled up with fog again. And I watched Leah and Vic wandering around in their own clouds. But we touched each other's face or hands or shoulders in passing now. Vic took a walk. Leah fixed breakfast. I washed dishes almost as if it were any slow blue sunday.

But when my old bug putted back up the driveway around noon, the sight of Jill brought everything into focus. I almost said, oh no, out loud when she unfolded from the driver's seat wearing some piece of black crepe finery. The worst part was the makeup, which I suppose they consider elegant in the city. Out there in the woods it made her look like a clown. I said, "Jesus, Jill, where did you get that dress?"

She said, "My closet," with a sweet face that made me want to kick it in for fear I'd kiss it if I didn't. And she let her hair out of the intricate bun she had piled it in on top of her head.

"You can't wear it for the ceremony," I said quietly.

She said, "I know." But she only leaned over and reached into the passenger seat, brought out a gold cookie tin trimmed with roses and started into the farmhouse.

Vic was arranging flowers in the livingroom. When she looked up at Jill, I saw betrayal chasing recognition across her face. It made me wish I had held Jill down and scrubbed her face. Vic gave me a glance that said, straight women, I swear, you think they understand and then they show up dressed to kill. To Jill, she whistled low and said, with all the sarcasm a softspoken woman can muster, "Did you bring cookies?"

But Jill just kept walking right up to Leah who stood in the kitchen doorway with her weight balanced for battle and her arms crossed. Jill pressed the tin into Leah's hands and said, "No, It's Carol."

I shivered. Leah's moss brown eyes registered shock and completion. Vic rubbed her head and sat down. Sometimes that sister of mine amazes me.

As soon as I could formulate the question I asked, "How did you get her?"

Jill sank into the rocker and kicked off one high heel and then the other. I forgave the innocence with which she said, "I've been getting things I wasn't supposed to have for a long time. I just walked into the mortuary and asked for her. The trick is to look as if you belonged there."

I said, "Oh, goddess. What happens when her family shows up to collect her?" I wasn't going to stop and say, of course, we're her real family. I knew by then Jill knew what I meant.

She said, "That won't be any problem. I made a switch and took the urn back and told them I'd made a terribly embarrassing mistake picking up the wrong one at the wrong place. I don't think they'll tell Carol's parents they almost gave it to a complete stranger."

Something in the way Leah held the tin verified Jill's claim. That and a quiver I'd always felt whenever I contemplated touching Carol. Back in the city I knew Carol's parents' plane was lifting off for Pittsburgh. Jill was stretching those long legs out with all of her terrible confidence. And I knew all she wanted was for me to ask, "Okay, what's in their urn?"

She arched a pencilled eyebrow, reached over and tapped the top of the cold stove and said, "Ashes."

CONTRIBUTORS' NOTES

Carole A. Carr was born in Blackpool, England, in 1945. She is currently studying anthropology at the University of Washington in Seattle and thinks humor is the best antidote to life.

Susan Doro was born in 1937 and lives in Oakland, California, where she is executive director of Tradeswoman, Inc., a national organization of women in nontraditional blue collar jobs. She previously lived in Milwaukee and worked for twelve years as a machinist. Her publications include two books of poetry, *Of Birds and Factories*, and *Heart, Home, and Hardhats.*

Kenyatta Koontz is currently residing in Seattle, Washington, where she has recently completed trade school and hopes soon to be once more gainfully employed. She enjoys horseback riding, running, and painting, and looks forward to returning to school to pursue a career in alternative medicine. *Commencement* is her first published story.

Marian Michener lives in Seattle, Washington, where she is an academic advisor at the UW. She has an M.A. in creative writing from SFSU and has had short stories and reviews published in *Common Lives/Lesbian Lives, Rag Times, Lesbian Contradiction,* and *Seattle Gay News.* She is currently working on a novel.

Carol Orlock was born in 1947 and lives in Seattle. She has an M.A. in creative writing from San Francisco State and teaches writing at the UW. She has a novel, *The Goddess Letters,* coming out in 1987 (St. Martin's Press). Her short stories have appeared in *Calyx, Clinton St. Quarterly, Backbone II,* and other publications.

Diana Rivers is a fifty-five-year-old lesbian-feminist, artist-writer, ex-New Yorker now living in the hills of Arkansas on women's land, in a house built by women's hands, including her own. She has been writing for about twelve years and has stories published in *Conditions, Sinister Wisdom, Feminary,* and the anthology *Lesbian Fiction.* Her full-length lesbian fantasy adventure story *Journey to Zelindar* will be published by Lace in 1987.

Ruthann Robson was born in 1956 and lives in Florida. Her work includes fiction, poetry, essays, criticism and "scholarship" and has been published in many periodicals and anthologies, including *Conditions, Room of One's Own, Trivia, Kalliope, IKON, Labyris, Speaking for Ourselves: Southern Women's Voices* (Pantheon, 1985) and forthcoming in *Early Ripening* (edited by Marge Piercy, Pandora). In addition to being a writer, she is an attorney, teacher, unwed mother, and relentless feminist.

Susan B. Strong lives in San Francisco, where she is an itinerant genetic engineer and massage therapist.